1500
670

W9-BII-819

Citizen Committees
A Guide to Their Use in Local Government

Citizen Committees

A Guide to Their Use in Local Government

Joseph Lee Rodgers, Jr.
Professor of Regional and City Planning
University of Oklahoma

Ballinger Publishing Company ● **Cambridge, Massachusetts**
A Subsidiary of J.B. Lippincott Company

This book is printed on recycled paper.

International Standard Book Number: 0-88410-654-3

Library of Congress Catalog Card Number: 76-56193

Printed in the United States of America

Library of Congress Cataloging in Publication Data

Rodgers, Joseph Lee.
  Citizen committees.

  Bibliography: p.
    1. Citizens' associations—United States.
  2. Local government—United States. 3. Political participation—
  United States. I. Title
  JS303.5.R6   322.4'3'06273   76-56193
  ISBN 0-88410-654-3

Contents

❋

Preface

During the past twenty years the League of Women Voters
of Norman, Oklahoma, as in many other cities, has spon-
sored a public forum prior to each local election. All candi-
dates are invited to respond, both in writing and orally, to a group of
carefully prepared questions, a process designed to illuminate both
personal knowledge and attitudes about public issues. Moreover,
League members have been active in studying a wide range of other
community issues, and have personally been politically active in the
general improvement of local government, the direct result of women
dedicated to collective, nonpartisan study and individual action. Significantly, this organized effort of a volunteer group of citizens, sustained over several decades, is not unique in terms either of sustained
commitment or of the community where it occurred.

Three San Francisco women initiated a movement in 1960 that
resulted in a new citizens' organization called the Save San Francisco
Bay Association. Rapid filling and pollution of the bay was threatening to destroy one of the city's most important aesthetic and economic assets. The action of the Association led to the creation of the
Bay Area Conservation and Development Commission in 1965 to
plan and enforce broad conservation measures, backed by new state
legislation.

In Chicago citizens organized the Clean Air Coordinating Committee to monitor air pollution and lobby for stricter laws and im-
proved enforcement.

These examples are typical of a pattern that has, for decades, been occurring in large cities, small towns, suburban areas and rural communities across America. Organizations of citizens of great variety and number have addressed and solved innumerable community problems. Some groups have been legally constituted by local government charter or ordinance—park boards, human rights commissions, environmental boards, library boards, planning commissions and boards of adjustment. Other citizen groups, such as project area committees and rural area development committees, were created in response to federal program requirements; while still others were initiated to represent the needs of special interest groups—neighborhood associations, tenant councils, work groups and business district development associations.

All of these citizen organizations have one common characteristic. Each has been conducted through the volunteer efforts of citizens who willingly participated in a common venture of mutual interest. This propensity for voluntary participation in the conduct of public affairs has been a hallmark of twentieth century local government in the United States. While much has been written on legally constituted citizen commissions and on the general subject of citizen participation, there is little to direct those who are responsible for organizing citizen committees.

This guide has been compiled to assist mayors and other city officials, students of planning, human relations and public administrators, members of the League of Women Voters, Chamber of Commerce executives, U.S. Department of Agriculture personnel, and other public officials and private citizens who are responsible for creating or participating on citizen committees. It is largely based on my personal experiences gained in working as a professional city planner with city councils, planning commissions, chambers of commerce and a variety of citizens committees. Begun in 1946, this work has been conducted during the past thirty years in more than forty metropolitan areas, cities, small towns and rural committees in Oklahoma and throughout the Southwest.

I am especially appreciative of the opportunity to observe the community organization efforts of many highly successful public officials and professionals in local government. Particularly noteworthy has been the work of the late Stanley Draper, past secretary-manager of the Oklahoma City Chamber of Commerce. Other significant contributors include W.P. Fowler, Irvin Hurst, James N.

Miles, Robert W. Quinlan, Frank Sneed, Robert Wegner and three of my close associates in teaching and planning practice, Richard N. Kuhlman, Robert L. Lehr and Charles R. Goins. My thanks go to Jess Abrams who contributed the information on the Project Area Committee that is included in this work. I am also indebted to Melvin B. Mogulof for his perceptive writings on citizen participation. Acknowledgment is made of Jane Hisey who cheerfully typed many initial drafts of this work, and of Betty Bellis who typed the final copy of the manuscript. Finally, my special appreciation is expressed to my wife for her constant companionship and encouragement, and for her careful editing of the final manuscript.

This work is dedicated to all citizen volunteers, everywhere, who work on committees, commissions, boards and associations involved in the public work of America. May their numbers and their efforts multiply.

J.L.R.

Citizen Committees
A Guide to Their Use in Local Government

Chapter 1

Introduction

Citizen participation in governmental affairs was a founding principle of democratic self-government in the United States, and it remains an important tenet of local government today. This proclivity for personal involvement in public affairs has been viewed by citizens as warranted on its own merits. It has not been justified because it is more efficient, economical or convenient. It may contribute all, or none, of these valued operational characteristics in given situations. Indeed, the idea of a free and open process for conducting the public's business, with every citizen not only having the right to know but also the responsibility to be intelligently involved, has been deemed inherently desirable. A government "of the people, by the people, and for the people" is a government of citizen participation.

The variety of citizen responses in public affairs has been wide-ranging. Citizens have run for public office; lobbied for their special interests; obtained writs of mandamus to force public officials to act; taken legal action to halt pollution; worked directly in conservation, beautification and other community projects; established public information and education programs; invoked economic sanctions including boycotts; served on citizen committees, and generally responded as if each held a very personal and proprietary interest in what government was doing.

More than a century ago Alexis de Tocqueville wrote of this characteristic of Americans to voluntarily associate for common purposes. "Wherever at the head of some new undertaking you see the government in France, or a man of rank in England, in the United States, you will be sure to find an association."[1]

One has only to view the almost endless list of citizen committees, councils and associations at work in American communities at any one time to realize the intensity of interest and involvement of citizens in different aspects of local affairs. A recent study of agencies responsible for one function, that of health care, in an Oklahoma county having a 1970 population of 35,358 identified some thirty-two different volunteer citizen organizations which were directly or indirectly responsible for some aspect of health care in the community.[2]

The broad range of functions for which citizen committees have been organized includes the development of public goals and policies, initiating or implementing specific public programs, advising official public agencies and performing specific tasks. In addition, commitees have also been concerned with reviewing public agency performance, providing opportunity for study and education on public issues, establishing a mechanism for increased minority participation, and organizing to carry out special interest objectives.

For a variety of reasons, citizen committees have had an increasingly prominent role in public affairs in the twentieth century. A large amount of citizen participation was mandated by various federal categorical grant programs of the 1960s including urban renewal, model cities and the Office of Economic Opportunity. Much of this was conducted through a citizen committee structure. While most of these categorical programs have been replaced by the block grant concept, implemented through revenue sharing and other means, the Community Development Act of 1974 also requires citizen participation under the Community Development Block Grant Program.[3]

The act stipulates that citizens are to be provided with information on funds, activities and programs through public hearings and other means. Methods for citizen participation are not specifically delineated in the law but are left to the discretion of local governments. Undoubtedly extensive use will be made of citizen committees in community development block grant programs. A publication of the National Model Cities Community Development Directors Association recommends the use of neighborhood advisory committees, subcommittees and task forces as part of the citizen participation mechanism.[4]

While much recent discussion of citizen participation has focused on citizen committees involved in urban renewal, model cities and other programs in large urban centers, some of the greatest benefits of citizen involvement have occurred in small towns and rural communities. Indeed, the very nature of these smaller human settlements makes them ideally suited for volunteer citizen efforts. The small urban center has certain liabilities, inherent in being small, that can be at least partially alleviated by organized group efforts.

First, the small city has a limited and less diversified economic base than larger urban centers and, therefore, is more deeply influenced by sudden changes in the local, regional and national economies. A change in the level of employment in a large local factory or one crop failure in the county will be felt throughout the entire community.

Second, any major external change will tend to have significant influence on the whole city. The addition of 500 residents to a town of 5,000 during a one year period would radically affect the purchasing power, cost of housing and demand for municipal services.

Third, the social pressures of a small city make it more difficult to establish and administer various codes and ordinances which are needed to protect the general environment and insure good quality construction. Building, plumbing and electrical codes; housing and zoning ordinances; antipollution and antilittering regulations; and health and sanitation ordinances are necessary for the preservation of life and property within every community. They become difficult to enforce when a violator is a friend, a neighbor or a business associate.

Finally, the management, engineering, planning and other technical manpower for dealing with problems usually is limited. The chief executive of a large city can call upon a well-trained professional staff to prepare plans for water and sewer extensions or open space and recreation programs. In a small community, the same problems are left to the ingenuity often of a single administrator, an outside consultant or a volunteer citizen committee.

Conformance to standards or norms in a small town tends to be achieved through voluntary community consensus and the indirect social pressures growing out of frequent personal encounters, rather than by the direct coercive enforcement of ordinances that is typical in large cities. Often it is not a major issue but the accumulation of the numerous unsolved small problems that greatly detracts from the quality of life in a small community. Matters that are routinely handled in a large city—such as cleaning streets, painting traffic lanes, repairing traffic control devices, codifying and printing ordinances, updating maps and reproducing records, reviewing subdivision plats, and scheduling road maintenance—may be chronic problems for small cities.

The development and conduct of public programs in small communities frequently rests more on the initiative of individual citizens and organized citizen groups than on the formal administrative structure of government agencies. The importance of these organized citizen groups as vehicles for community action in small towns was identified by Arthur Vidich and Joseph Bensman. "It is characteristic of community life that a heavy emphasis is placed upon organized group activities. Such organizations, of which in a strict accounting there are more than two hundred (in the small town of Springdale, New York, with a population of 2,500), serve a wide range of purposes and functions."[5] Many, but not all of these organized groups, were created as citizen committees, in the form of study or work groups to review or carry out some community project. The frequent face-to-face encounters of people working together in a group, and committed to a common purpose, tends to be a unifying community effort and provides an important informal mechanism of social control in the small community. In fact, much of the success of the U.S. Department of Agriculture in greatly improving farming practices and the general quality of rural life during the twentieth century can be attributed to the astute involvement of rural citizens in both the conduct and support of a wide range of activities. A brief resume of more than forty years of this volunteer citizen effort illustrates the diversity and the importance of the achievements resulting from citizen participation in public affairs.

Programs for rural America that were developed in response to the Agricultural Adjustment Act of 1933 were based on the concept of citizen cooperation and voluntary participation. This new experiment in grassroots democracy in agriculture was described by M.L. Wilson, director of extension work in 1940, as embracing the following principles:

1. Decentralized administration in varying degrees through community, county and state farmer committees, elected by cooperating farmers or appointed by the secretary of agriculture.
2. The use of referendums in determining certain administrative

policies, especially those having to do with quotas, penalties and marketing agreements.

3. The use of group discussion and other adult education techniques as a means of promoting understanding of the problems and procedures involved in administration of the various programs and referendums.

4. Cooperative planning in program formulation and localization of programs.[6]

Large numbers of rural citizens became actively involved in local agricultural adjustment committees, county land use committees, local committees of the Farm Security Administration, local district advisory boards for the grazing service and many other types of voluntary associations. It was reported that in 1940, ". . . over 890,000 citizens were helping to plan and operate nine rural action programs: community, county, and state committees of the Agricultural Adjustment Administration, operating through over 3,000 county agricultural associations; . . ."[7]

This same emphasis on grassroots democracy through citizen participation was one of the basic tenets of the Tennessee Valley Authority program. The TVA legislation was an experiment in combining the vast power and resources of the federal government with the initiative and energy of local people. The benefits resulting from this local-federal partnership has been described by Gordon R. Clapp.[8] "In a short time we rid ouselves of the temptation and the opportunity to wield authority over the individual farmer on his own land. The result was to release a great reserve of local initiative in community after community. Ideas we might never have developed came from the people and were put to the test in their local programs."[9]

Following the successful experiments in citizen participation in the 1930s, the USDA has continued to effectively involve farmers on local Agricultural Stabilization Commission (ASC) committees and local Soil Conservation Service (SCS) committees to establish and carry out local USDA policies and programs.

The substantial successes of early programs to improve farm production and marketing of products changed agriculture from labor intensive, frequently subsistence level farming to a highly mechanized activity. This trend has accelerated during the past four decades and has caused a major reduction in the rural labor force.

These major shifts in agriculture obviously required changes in USDA and other programs. The poverty and unemployment that gripped the nation in the 1930s remained strikingly high in rural areas in the years following World War II. In rural territory outside of metropolitan counties, 23 percent of all households were living below the poverty level in 1967. At the same time, in small cities and towns 19 percent lived in poverty, compared to 16 percent for metropolitan central cities and 9 percent for their suburbs.[10] Responding to the problems of declining rural America, a variety of federal programs were developed, to be administered by the Department of Agriculture, the Department of Commerce, the Department of Housing and Urban Development, and the Office of Economic Opportunity. Citizen participation was a major component and a basic operational strategy of each federal agency.[11]

New programs of the USDA focused on rural development in the early 1950s. These included credit programs, vocational training, health programs and job placement through state employment services.[12] USDA activities were expanded under the Kennedy administration in 1962 with the creation of Rural Area Development (RAD) committees in designated counties. These local citizen committees were assigned responsibility for preparing "overall economic development programs" (OEDPs) working closely with the county extension agent. The membership on these "OEDP committees," as they were commonly known, was not limited to farmers, since the post-1961 policies of USDA explicitly encouraged nonfarm participation in rural development programs.[13] This was necessary as increasing numbers of farm families moved to small towns, but continued to farm, and larger numbers of city people moved to suburban and rural tracts, but continued to commute to jobs in urban centers. Economic and social interests of rural and urban groups were becoming increasingly mixed and interrelated and had to be reflected in programs for rural development. The OEDP citizen committee formed one of the principle vehicles for bringing together these newly developing coalitions to act on common problems.

It seems evident that citizen committees have formed an important mechanism for citizen participation throughout all levels of government for a long period in American history, and their use and value continues to increase. In recent years they have proved effective in increasing minority involvement, and they seem uniquely suited to sustaining contact between government officials and the "grass roots." The general subject of citizen participation has received considerable attention in contemporary literature, yet specific studies of citizen committees have been far more limited.[14]

Although there are many thousands of committees composed of citizens who devote millions of hours of work each year to a wide variety of projects and issues, there is a dearth of opportunities for formal training and little published literature on the subject.

Executives and elected public officials who are responsible for working with citizen groups seldom receive instruction on the objectives, strategies and criteria for constituting and utilizing committees for citizen participation. Those who work with citizen committees are largely dependent upon their own experiences, intuition and the informal exchange of ideas with other officials. This is frequently a cause of frustration among citizens whose committee roles are ill-defined, and among administrators and policymakers who feel that committees often become involved in irrelevant or politically embarrassing issues for which they were not assigned responsibility. An understanding of the types, purposes and organizational characteristics of citizen committees is a prerequisite to effective citizen participation.

Chapter 2

Citizen Committees Characterized

There are a variety of ways in which citizen committees may be defined and characterized, each of which will indicate different methods by which they may effectively contribute to public programs. Committees may be typed according to the parent organizational unit that creates the committee, by the organizational unit or constituency to which the committee is responsible and by the primary function of the committee. Following a general definition, each of these is discussed briefly to indicate the different forms which may be taken by a particular committee.

CITIZEN COMMITTEES DEFINED

The following factors normally characterize or define a citizen committee:

1. Citizens serve voluntarily, usually without monetary compensation, though members are normally reimbursed for expenses, and when minority participation is involved, small stipends may be paid. There are other types of rewards, however, in the form of public recognition, prestige and advanced access to privileged information.
2. Work of committee members is on a part-time basis only, even though the committee may be either ad hoc (temporary) or have continuing responsibilities.

3. Membership may be by appointment, in an ex officio capacity, or through election from a citizen's interest group.
4. The committee member roles and responsibilities are either specified by the appointing authority or by the committee itself, but, unlike the legally constituted citizen commission, the committee "charge" is not specified by law. The creation of the committee may be mandated by a law or an administrative ruling, however, as illustrated by the many local citizen committees created in response to federal urban renewal programs.

CITIZEN COMMITTEES CONTRASTED WITH LEGALLY CONSTITUTED CITIZEN COMMISSION

In order to distinguish between a citizen committee, as described above, and legally constituted citizen commissions and boards that are deeply involved in local government affairs, these legal commissions are briefly characterized. Local government commissions are permanent standing committees, legally created by a local charter or ordinance that defines the scope of their powers and responsibilities. They may be organized to provide advice on policy matters, to administer programs or to act in quasi-judicial review and fact-finding roles. Special knowledge, a capacity for leadership and an interest in the area of concern constitute the principle requirements for membership.

Examples of these legally formed citizen groups include planning commissions; boards of adjustment; human rights and community relations commissions; environmental commissions; hospital, library, park, airport and utility boards; and housing and urban renewal boards. Citizen commissions may be appointed to deal with new and controversial areas of public concern or issues for which no previous organizational pattern has been established. This use of a citizen commission also may insulate the legislative body from issues for which a politically oriented city councilman does not want direct responsibility.

Appointment is normally on a nonpartisan basis for a definite term, usually three to four years. Continuity may be provided through use of overlapping terms that do not coincide with the term of office of the elected appointing authority. Those who have rendered effective service often are reappointed. Members are usually appointed by the mayor in consultation with members of the city council. They will be expected to spend considerable time and effort in one to four official meetings each month and in group and independent study of issues at other times.

Newly created commissions may be responsible for hiring their own staff and may need both resident personnel and consultants. As the role of the commission becomes more clearly defined and permanent, there will be a tendency for staff to be integrated into the administrative structure of local government where it will be subject to normal hiring procedures and responsible to the chief executive officer of the city.

There is considerable similarity between legally constituted commissions and voluntary citizen committees. Members of both groups serve on a part-time basis only, and normally without monetary compensation. To be effective, each must have knowledgeable and interested participants. There are enough similarities in roles and responsibilities that service on a voluntary citizen committee constitutes good training and frequently is a stepping stone to work on the more complex official boards and commission.

ORGANIZATIONAL UNIT WHICH
CREATES THE COMMITTEE

The role and purposes of many citizen committees, particularly those used traditionally in local government, have been largely shaped by the appointing authority—the mayor, the city council or a functional agency. Experiences of local committees established to administer USDA programs, and recent studies that have examined citizen committee roles in the Office of Economic Opportunity (OEO), urban renewal and model cities programs, however, suggest that citizen interest groups have been increasingly active in shaping committee activities. There is evidence that federal policies that have required citizen participation have substantially expanded the purposes and the influence of citizen committees in public policymaking and program administration.[1] Initiative and involvement of local people are spreading through new types of committee structures and roles, thereby extending power and control of citizen groups, often at the expense of local government agencies. This sharing of power among a broader range of minority and other groups via citizen committees probably is a healthy trend in local self-government.

While local public officials continue to create and use many types of committees, the trend toward citizen-initiated committees may also increase. Several different types of organizational units involving either public officials or private individuals or both may create a citizen committee. The following is a summary of four different types of initiating units:

1. Individuals or a coalition of existing groups in the community may coalesce around an issue of common interest. A health service committee composed of representatives from several ethnic minorities and from health professionals is illustrative of this type of committee.
2. A committee may be created by a local legislative body, public official or government agency to give advice, or to administer or develop programs for which the parent agency is responsible. City councils and mayors have created a great variety of general and technical advisory committees, policy review committees, citizen councils and other similar groups.
3. The power structure of the community may form a committee to carry out a specific program or activity. This may take the form of an economic or industrial development committee or a regional council.
4. A citizen interest group may organize for a specific objective. Neighborhood associations and downtown improvement associations are representative of this type of committee.

Committees that are created by public agencies normally are public issue oriented, while those generated out of citizens' interest groups or the power structure may involve public issues, but tend to be more self-interest or special interest centered. This distinction between public and special interest should not infer a value judgment. Indeed, the public interest in a pluralistic society frequently may be best served by a system that is sensitive to the many minority and other special interest groups in a community. It may be that democracy works most effectively when there is tension among various subgroups which gives visibility to different positions and forces a more complete justification of choices among competing alternatives.

The public interest is a difficult idea with which to deal, and may lead to a variety of misconceptions. The term is employed to distinguish between public and proprietary concerns, yet an action taken in the public interest does not necessarily benefit all citizens equally. A reduction of air pollution in the region may have universal public benefits, while the construction of a new storm drain or a public tennis center has benefits limited by both territory and interest.

The public interest may be explained more clearly in terms of the interests of several publics. These different publics are essentially special interest groups. Depending on the issue, some groups will have common interests and some will be competing, but on most public programs levels of interest will differ among citizen groups. The coalitions of interest groups that dominate in influencing goverment institutions largely dictate which special interests will benefit most significantly from governmental action. The differential benefits that result from public action are, in fact, a primary motivation for citizen involvement in public affairs, and probably are one of the principle causes for the recent upsurge in minority participation in citizen committee activities.

The direct involvement of minority representation in policy making is noted by Mogulof:

> ... it is easier to influence the making of policy when one controls the policy apparatus than by pursuing that apparatus from the outside. And this may be what citizen participation is really all about; changing the composition of policy-making bodies so that the aggrieved elements of our society have representation *inside*, where decisions affecting them are being made.[2]

This search for a larger share of the "action" has led many special interest groups, minorities and others, to take the initiative in organizing citizen committees. Watchdog, preparative and advisory committees have proved to be effective mechanisms for direct as well as indirect intervention in policymaking. It might be expected, therefore, that citizens will continue to create committees to become directly involved in policy and program development and administration and to preempt some of the powers of established agencies through administrative, advisory and watchdog committees. As a countermeasure, established agencies may take the initiative in creating advisory committees in an effort to assure "friendly" advisors. In such cases, however, the appointing authority cannot be assured of maintaining control of its creation, since committees tend to develop their own unique personalities that may at times operate rather independently of the parent organization.

ORGANIZATION OR CONSTITUENCY
TO WHICH THE COMMITTEE
IS RESPONSIBLE

The group or agency initiating a committee may retain considerable control of its membership and reporting procedure, or it may relinquish substantial power to the committee by giving it independent responsibility to initiate action. Committees once created may or may not remain responsible to the creating unit, but they always have a constituency to whom they are accountable.

In many instances a citizen committee may remain responsible to those creating it. This is usually true of advisory committees appointed by city councils to give feedback on policies and programs. Conversely, a city council may create a planning or administrative committee and provide for substantial committee autonomy. In such instances the committee normally is responsible to a citizen constituency, frequently one composed of consumers for whom it provides a program or service, as exemplified by committees administering legal aid and health programs to minorities.

Committees may be responsible to a citizens' interest group from which they have been appointed or elected. This applies both to committees with representatives from disadvantaged minorities and to those generated out of the power structure and other elitist groups. A neighborhood association may be created at the instigation of a public agency or by local citizen action, but it is responsible for reporting to and serving the interests of the citizens of the neighborhood that it represents.

The relationship between a committee and its constituency has a direct bearing on the effectiveness of a committee. In fact, there is considerable evidence to indicate that the power of a committee member is directly proportional to the political power of the constituency represented. The importance of a constituency is noted by Mogulof: "It should be apparent that a representative speaks with a much louder voice . . . when it is clear that one speaks for others as well as one's self."[3]

While those who make up the power structure of a community may exercise control of economic resources, their major political influence comes from an ability to represent and lead a broad constituency; and conversely, the more influential the constituency the greater the power of those who represent it. The increased voice and political power of ethnic minorities in the United States in recent years undoubtedly has resulted from coalitions of small groups to form broader and more militant constituencies that provide a strong power base for minority leaders. This unification of constituencies formed the political base around which increased community action could be taken. "A constituency which periodically comes together and functions as a collectivity or people is an aspect of an organized community."[4] The opposite is equally true. Where no interest group can be identified to which a leader is accountable, there is no basis for organized action, and a general absence of community. Indeed, a committee composed of members without significant constituencies is merely an exercise in token participation.

COMMITTEES CHARACTERIZED BY PRIMARY FUNCTIONS

Most citizen committees are created to serve one or more primary functions, and also may have several other significant but somewhat secondary purposes. A citizen council may be appointed by the mayor to develop policies and programs for city improvement and to advise on other community issues. It may form a channel for participation of ethnic and other minorities. It is difficult to distinguish the most important functions of the committee among the several significant roles that it may serve. Yet it is clearly useful to identify separate functions if the scope of responsibility of a particular committee is to be established.

A reiteration of the activities with which citizen committees are frequently involved includes developing public policies, initiating or implementing specific public programs, advising on public issues and carrying out tasks. Other purposes with which committees are concerned involve reviewing public agency performance, providing opportunity for study and education, creating a mechanism for increasing minority participation and organizing to carry out special interest objectives. These different areas of concern have been grouped into several separate categories, one or more of which form the functional responsibilities of most citizen committees as follows:

1. **Administration Committees:** *Policy and program administration committees.* These committees tend to be quasi-governmental in that they are created to operate programs of an ad hoc or continuous

nature that are relatively new, and that have not yet been incorporated as a local government department or board. Committees formed to administer health, recreation and legal services programs fall into this category, as do local ASC committees.

2. **Advisory Committees:** *Goals, policies, plan, program or personnel advisory committees.* These committees study and give advice on public issues, but are not responsible for the actual preparation of policies or programs. General and technical advisory committees, and in some cases citizen councils, are representative of this category.

3. **Minority Participation Committees:** *Administrative, advisory, preparative, review and special purpose committees.* Many committees were mandated under federal programs to increase minority involvement in public issues, including urban renewal, project area committees (PAC) and public housing tenants councils.

4. **Preparative Committees:** *Goals, policies, plan, program preparation committees.* These committees have responsibility for the actual preparation of public programs and include planning committees, rural area development committees, community goals committees, community councils and task forces.

5. **Review Committees:** *Review of policy implementation or actions of public officials.* These committees are commonly referred to as watchdog committees and are expressly charged with reviewing actions of governmental agencies or officials to see that public actions are in accord with standards of performance acceptable to the constituency of the committee.

6. **Special Purpose Committees:** *Those representing coalitions of common interest groups formed for special purposes.* Coalitions such as neighborhood associations, central business district associations, and industrial and area development commissions may be formed by private citizens having mutual interests. Memberships may also represent coalitions of government agencies or combinations of government agencies and private interest groups. Included in this list are community action agency boards (established in response to the Economic Development Act of 1964 and subsequent OEO programs), citizen councils of some types, some metropolitan councils and metropolitan associations of public officials.

7. **Task Performance Committees:** *Groups organized to carry out specific public projects.* A wide variety of specific tasks and projects are carried out by community work groups and task forces. Activities are usually of an ad hoc nature and may range from the simple job of

cleaning litter from public streets to the highly complex task of evaluation of the economic development requirements of state government. Small projects involving limited numbers of participants usually are referred to as work groups while more complex tasks requiring larger numbers of people are called task forces.

These characteristics of citizen committees, set forth above, do not indicate, however, the depth of citizen involvement in community decisionmaking and the conduct of public programs. Some committees are given power to initiate action, control resources and provide advice on significant public issues. Others go through a ritual of participation but have no real influence on the outcome of issues. In a study of citizen committees used in urban renewal, antipoverty and model cities programs, Sherry R. Arnstein developed a typology of eight levels of citizen participation, ranging from nonparticipation to full involvement. This "ladder of citizen participation" indicated degrees of citizen power that started at the bottom as "manipulation" and "therapy" levels at which citizens were used in contrived ways as a substitute for real involvement. "Partnership," "delegated power" and full "citizen control" formed the upper end of the ladder and represented highly significant citizen roles in decisionmaking.[5]

If citizen committees are to be an effective channel for full participation in public programs it is evident that members will need to have more than token roles. This does not mean that committees will need a large degree of autonomy for effective work. In fact, most committees are created to assist in, but not control, the decisionmaking process in which they participate. Effective participation does not necessarily mean direct citizen control, but it does require respect for the integrity of the principle of participation. There are both benefits and problems that may result from the work of voluntary citizen committees. These assets and liabilities are summarized in the next chapter.

Chapter 3

Advantages and Problems Attributed to the Use of Citizen Committees

As an inherent part of American local government, citizen participation at some levels of decisionmaking has assured greater sensitivity and equity in the development of public programs. In other situations factionalism and partisan political actions have slowed or stopped important public projects. As instruments of citizen participation, the activities of citizen committees have also produced both positive and negative social consequences. An examination of the benefits and detriments attributed to citizen committees, as organizational units, should give some indication as to when and how committees can be used most effectively.

BENEFITS ATTRIBUTED TO THE USE OF CITIZEN COMMITTEES

A wide variety of benefits have been ascribed to the employment of citizen committees, though these may vary with different types of committees. A summary of potentially desirable effects that may result from utilizing citizen committees includes the following:

1. Use of citizen committees should increase public access to the decisionmaking process, thereby expanding interest in and understanding of public issues. This broadening of public knowledge should improve the ability of the community to equitably distribute power and public resources. Self-determinism in local affairs should be strengthened.

2. Committees serve as effective informational and educational channels to "grassroots" constituencies. A greater citizen consciousness of public programs and plans should result, and in turn provide feedback that would permit public programs to reflect sensitively individual and local needs.

3. Participation in committee work provides excellent education on public issues and gives many citizens greater insight into the difficulties inherent in the public decisionmaking process.

4. Elected officials will tend to be more responsive to the electorate since citizen review of issues tends to improve deliberation, expand press coverage, and increase the number of alternatives that may be considered. This "opening up" of the process should reduce partisanship in decisionmaking and expand official accountability, thereby increasing the possibilities of implementation once policies have been officially adopted.

5. A greater involvement of knowledgeable citizens should generate new ideas and increase innovation and creativity in developing and implementing public programs.

6. A citizens committee (frequently in the form of a technical advisory committee) is a useful mechanism through which to channel special talent to benefit public programs. Citizens with unique knowledge or skills have the right to expect that their advice will be given special weight on issues where their expertise is relevant.

7. Citizens committees serve as important vehicles for increasing minority involvement and leadership training in public issues. Many socially and economically disadvantaged people have been given their first chance to influence public policies affecting their neighborhoods through service on tenants councils, project area committees and neighborhood associations.

8. Committees may provide channels of cooperation and communication among people of different backgrounds who have common interests. Coalitions of minority constituencies may unify efforts on issues of common concern through a citizen committee. Aggregation of power may extend across political boundaries, neighborhood lines or ethnic groups to generate support for a single program of common interest. This has frequently been illustrated in the operation of committees concerned with the delivery of health services.

9. Citizen committee efforts often make the exercise of political

power more visible and bring issues into sharper focus. This increased public deliberation may result in the polarization of opinions and force decisions, thereby reducing lethargy in official actions.

10. A committee may establish a forum where ideas and concepts can be tested and where legitimate differences of opinion can be resolved. A general advisory committee often has been used as a mechanism through which representatives from competing factions can chose from several alternatives and agree upon a single course of action.

11. As an instrument for generating cooperation between private sector and public sector leaders, a committee may guide the use of private resources toward public purposes.

12. Legitimacy may be given to local, state and federal programs that might, without citizen committee input, lack credibility.

The above factors have been classified as advantages based on the assumption that the broadest possible citizen involvement in public decisions at the local level—neighborhood, town, city, country and metropolitan—is inherently desirable. Obviously not all of the work of all the citizen committees is beneficial when measured in public interest terms, however, and a review of some of the potential problems attending committee efforts is warranted.

PROBLEMS ASSOCIATES WITH THE
USE OF CITIZEN COMMITTEES

There is a relatively wide range of possible adverse consequences from citizen committee use. Not all problems are necessarily inherent in the committee system, but may result from ineffective or misuse of committees. A summary of possible problems includes the following:

1. Use of citizen committees may reduce consideration of the needs of minorities and reinforce biases toward existing norms if appointments are made from citizens representing the same social and economic status as that of the appointing authority.

2. The appearance of increased citizen involvement and support may be given, when in fact there may be only token participation, if citizen committee membership is unrepresentative of the various constituencies within the community. This is a special

problem in large metropolitan areas with many subcommunities, competing interest groups and low visibility constituencies—ethnic minorities, the aged, the young and the poor.

3. Use of citizen committees may increase conflicts if the work of committee members is largely ignored or rejected, or membership may be co-opted for purposes for which the committee was not created.

4. Vested interest groups may control or dominate a particular committee for self-serving purposes, thereby decreasing rather than spreading the power base.

5. A committee may absorb a large amount of technical staff time for lower level, less productive work than would otherwise be performed. Larger communities often establish a "special projects staff" in the planning agency to work on committee projects and special assignments from public officials. Greater competition for staff time occurs in smaller cities where professional and technical personnel must perform in a wider range of roles.

6. Committees may screen the city council from contact with professional staff, thereby reducing the educational benefits to legislators. Official citizen commissions pose a special threat of this nature. Issues may be studied and debated for several weeks by a planning commission, recommendations may be forwarded to the city council with only a short written explanation. The expanded knowledge and insight that results from staff–planning commissioner study and discussion is not received by the council. The result is that council members who were required to make the final policy decisions have less knowledge of the issues than their citizen advisors on the planning commission. The in-depth study of issues by individual members of a committee should be in addition to, and not a substitute for, an equally careful assessment by the members of the parent agency or public officials to whom the committee is responsible.

Citizen committees, because they are voluntary and meet intermittently, may seem to slow the legislative process unnecessarily. This problem can be reduced through staff support and open communications between committee leadership and public officials. No claim can be made that citizen involvement in a public decisionmaking effort is efficient or brings the process to a rapid conclusion, though acceleration of action may occasionally result. It can be argued, however, that more sensitive and equitable decisions result from greater deliberation growing out of citizen involvement; and this more than offsets any inherent slowness that may occur. To avoid problems and increase the probability of success of citizen committees, certain basic principles should guide their creation and use.

Chapter 4

Principles to Guide the Use of Citizen Committees

Successful citizen committee performance is influenced by the attitude, knowledge and ability of the appointing authority in constituting the committee. The linkage between public officials, both elected and appointed, and citizen committees created to work with them involves highly sensitive organizational relationships. Prerogatives of power and responsibility may be delicately balanced between a city council concerned with political survival and a nonpartisan citizen committee appointed to provide advice on highly controversial issues such as human relations, environmental protection or community aesthetics. Failure of the appointing authority to understand the abilities and limitations of citizen participation through committee structures and to reflect these constraints in the use of committees may negate any possible success before the committee starts to work.

The relationship between committee members and their constituencies is also critical. Some members are elected directly from a particular neighborhood and represent and report to a specific constituency. This is frequently the case with tenant councils and project area committees. In other situations, members may be appointed to represent communitywide interests, such as those appointed to serve on a policy advisory committee created by the city council. Members need to represent many different community groups, some with whom they do not have direct contact. In other cases, committee members may be appointed to administer programs that channel funds or services to minority consumer groups. Whether directly elected, or appointed to represent a constituency, to be effective committee members should understand the needs of those they represent and have credibility as their representatives. Persons may be elected or appointed from leaders who are indigenous members of a constituency, or they may be selected as advocates for a group, even though they are not members of the community whose interest they represent. When a member is selected to serve in an advocacy role, it is usually because a specialized talent is needed, as illustrated by the offering of legal aid or health services through a citizen committee structure. The use of knowledgeable professionals in such cases is mandatory, but it is equally necessary to select advocates who are sensitive to the needs of the group that they represent and who are acceptable to a large majority of those who compose the constituency. The constituting of a committee, including the method of membership selection, requires great care and an intimate knowledge of the internal structure of the community, to assure effective representation. Committees without constituencies can have little ultimate effect on public issues.

The following specific principles should guide those who create, appoint, work with or serve on a citizen committee:

There must be a commitment to the belief that citizen committees make a difference in the quality of public programs. Those who create a committee and request that citizens give time and effort should be committed to the belief that citizens can make a real contribution to the situation, and should be prepared to accept and utilize citizen input. To give lip service to the concept of citizen participation by appointing a committee, but largely ignore the work or recommendations developed out of extensive citizen effort, will do a great disservice to the community. The hypocrisy of such tactics not only will tend to generate opposition from participating citizens to the issues involved, but it may also create a long-term disenchantment with other governmental activities that need citizen participation and support. Citizen participation through committees means willingly shared power on the part of public officials because they believe that citizen efforts contribute to the quality of public programs.

Committees must be carefully constituted to reflect their purposes. The size and composition of the committee should be consistent with the purposes and responsibilities of the committee. Committees tend to have special institutional lives that are individually unique.

The artful blending of the special talents and personalities of the participants will deeply influence the success of the committee. For instance, an individual who may be highly effective on a steering committee of fifty persons might be unproductive on an eight person technical advisory committee.

The Committee "charge," which outlines the purpose of the committee, should clearly define the precise scope and the limits of responsibility of the committee. If possible, the charge of committee responsibility should be given verbally by the mayor or other appointing authority at the initial organization meeting, then reiterated by providing each member with a written statement. Not only should definite roles and expectations of the committee be clearly stated, but equally important may be a clear definition of the limits of responsibility. This setting of limits is particularly necessary when committees are involved in controversial policy issues. A citizens group that steps beyond the bounds of its charge may pose a real and often uncontrollable threat to other policy areas.

The committee should be provided with the resources needed to support effective work. The appointing authority should provide the committee with the staff, facilities, and monetary and other resources necessary to carry out assigned responsibilities. The type and amount of staff and other support will vary with each type of assignment. Frustration and ineffectiveness may result from committee attempts to deal with problems beyond the scope of committee time or ability. While committees should be provided with adequate resources to perform their work, permanent, exclusively used resources should normally not be assigned to ad hoc committees. This will reduce or avoid a tendency to form permanent but unneeded bureaucracies.

It should not be assumed that a citizen will be inherently effective in committee roles that may involve sensitive interpersonal relationships and specialized operational knowledge. Committees required to deal with technical programs or complex issues may need special training sessions for committee members. Staff resources, office space, meeting rooms and printed material should be provided to carry out these educational programs. The educational sessions may require contracting with industry, university, public agency or other sources for specialized talent to organize and conduct sessions.

Public meetings should be held in public places. All committees that are concerned with public interest issues, and particularly those appointed by the mayor or local legislative body, should hold all meetings in public buildings and have them open to the press. Public credibility suffers when public issues are dealt with in closed meetings or on proprietary turf, such as private conference rooms in banks or corporate meeting rooms. The neutral environment of a public conference room in a public building is normally the most appropriate place for deliberation on public issues. Study sessions may be held in other locations, especially where one or two day intensive sessions are involved. A retreat setting away from the community may be desirable, but the location and purpose of the sessions should be given advance publicity and the local press should be invited to participate and/or observe.

Social and employment patterns of minorities should be reflected in committee operations. When committees are established to increase participation from lower socioeconomic groups and ethnic minorities, the time and location of meetings will need to be scheduled to accommodate their work schedules and social patterns. Citizens who might feel alienated in a centrally located municipal building in a large city may be quite comfortable in a neighborhood school or recreation center. (The typical elementary school classroom with small-scale furniture is not, however, an appropriate facility.) In contrast to the general rule that citizens committee work is voluntary and without pay, it may be necessary to provide liberal compensation for transportation and other expenses, including stipends, to make possible participation of low income representation. Where stipends and expenses are provided, they should be given to all committee members. Payments restricted to those who make a personal declaration of need normally will not be utilized. Those in need frequently have too much pride to accept assistance requiring a personal statement of need.

Public recognition should be given to citizen committee members. The appointing authority should give public credit and recognition both to the efforts and the accomplishments of the committee. Citizens must feel that their work has been carefully considered and has made a contribution to the decisionmaking process if they are to continue to be of service and to provide support for public programs. Where extensive committee efforts have produced very limited results or have generated highly controversial proposals, recognition and appreciation of citizen effort rather than results can be emphasized.

Appointing authorities may find that proposals and recommendations of citizen committees need to be modified or even completely rejected by the local legislative body. This should be done only after due recognition of the committee efforts has been given and after careful and deliberate consideration of committee proposals. Perhaps nothing can cause as much disenchantment with local government as a city council's brusque and precipitous rejection of a citizen committee report on which considerable thought and time has been expended.

Citizen committees should not be used as a substitute for technical staff. This final principle, and one of the most important, relates to finances. Citizen committee volunteers should not be employed as a substitute for technical staff or in an attempt to acquire free professional services. Committee workers should not be used primarily to save the city the cost of hiring staff, although the projects carried out by task forces and work groups may result in substantial monetary savings. Volunteers cannot be expected to meet the major, long-term continuing requirements for providing community services for which professional and technical staff are needed.

An exception to this principle may occur in small towns and rural communities where the number of people with professional and technical skills is limited. In small human settlements, where individuals necessarily perform in a wider variety of both public and private roles than their counterparts in urban centers, the line between volunteer and monetarily compensated efforts cannot be as clearly drawn. More work of a communal nature may be conducted through formal committees or highly informal group efforts. Playgrounds are built, public buildings are painted and repaired, and libraries are started through volunteer citizen efforts in small communities. Even in these circumstances that evidence a strong community spirit, however, most of those public activities that are successful are of a short-term project nature. Programs requiring a long-term, continuous commitment of time and ability usually have succeeded only as a "labor of love" by one dedicated person. It may not be too difficult to generate broad voluntary support and contributions to start a small community library, but it is quite another problem to daily operate and add to library holdings over several decades. Even in small urban and rural communities, volunteer committee work can serve only as a limited substitute in selected situations for paid staff effort, given the social and economic patterns of contemporary American life.

When the first planning commissions were created by cities and towns under state enabling acts passed in the 1920s, businessmen, lawyers, architects, engineers and realtors predominated in appointments to these early commissions. The objective was to appoint members capable of making plans for the community. It was soon evident that plans could not be prepared by volunteer committees working only a few hours each week. Full-time staff was needed to make the necessary studies. Officials learned that planning commission members needed a capacity for leadership in planning and policymaking rather than an ability to make plans. This same principle applies to virtually all citizen standing committees and to ad hoc committees concerned with local government policy. The primary exceptions are those citizen committees that act in a fact-finding or review capacity, as illustrated by the work of human relations committees. While these require members with special knowledge, a farily limited time commitment is involved.

Citizens can make unique and special contributions through committee work because they have a proprietary feeling about the community and a strong emotional attachment to it. Their personal well-being is deeply intertwined with that of the community. Citizens may be flattered to be asked to serve in positions of leadership and consultation and may eagerly respond to positions requiring intensive effort and commitment. They should not be asked to serve in capacities that threaten their livelihood, however, either by giving professional services for which they normally receive compensation or by being placed in situations involving conflicts of interest. To illustrate, an engineer serving as a member of a technical advisory committee could effectively review flood plain zoning policies, but he should not be asked to contribute engineering plans for channel improvements in a local drainage basin. Citizen committee roles are different from staff work and should be in addition to, not as a substitute for, it.

Chapter 5

Individual Committee
Types Characterized

This material is organized as a guide for those responsible
for creating or serving on a citizen committee and for
students interested in committee characteristics. Not every
committee that is in use in the United States today will fit the typology or the descriptions used herein. Circumstances may dictate the
need for a committee that deviates from these characteristics. Innovation that contributes to increased citizen participation should be
encouraged, and this includes the creative use of citizen committees.
These committee descriptions, therefore, should not be treated as
norms that ought to be followed, but as guides that have proved useful in actual practice.

The discussion of each committee type is given under the headings: "Size and Composition," "Purpose and Organizational Characteristics," "Constituencies," and "Resource Support Required."
Figures on committee size do not indicate fixed limits but represent
the range generally prevalent in current practice.

Two types of constituencies are identified. Those persons, boards
or public officials to whom committee members directly report
form one type of constituency. This type may be a relatively small
board or city council, a large public organization such as a parent-
teachers association, or a special interest group concerned with area
redevelopment. In one sense these units to which committees directly report may be thought of as "parent" organizations rather than
true constituencies. In such cases a committee may be accountable

to, or may be created by, an agency without representing it, as evidenced by committees created to increase minority participation in policy development. Committees also may report to and represent the same group, thereby making it both a parent group and a constituency.

Amother type of constituency is one from which a committee member is considered to be a representative. In such situations, the member not only may be a participant, but also is frequently a leader of the group represented. Each committee member normally will belong to several formal and informal organizations in the community and will be perceived as representing several constituencies. Representation of some minority or special interest groups may take the form of a professional advocacy role, particularly where committees are responsible for service delivery to minority consumers. It is difficult to represent different groups with equal skill and commitment, however, since effective representation is dependent upon relatively complete and intimate knowledge of the desires and needs of the group represented and open channels of a two way communication. As the knowledge of and involvement with different constituencies varies, so will the ability to effectively speak for a group.

Those constituencies with which a committee member is intimately associated as a leader will be referred to as "primary constituencies." Those groups for whom the member speaks, but with more limited knowledge, will be referred to as "secondary constituencies." Most committee members will serve multiple constituencies, both primary and secondary. Constituencies concerned with the issues for which the committee is responsible need to be carefully identified and the membership of the committee constituted to give effective representation proportional to involvement of different interest groups. All committees have been classified under the typology developed earlier in this work. The more commonly used conventional names are employed for descriptions of individual committee types, and these specific names are included under one or more of the general headings most clearly depicting committee functions. In some cases the major headings and conventional names are identical. Variations in committee use has necessitated the inclusion of a name under more than one heading in a few instances. Committees by major classification and by convention names are as follows:

Administration Committees
Program or Service Administration Committee

Advisory Committees
Advisory Committee—General
Advisory Committee—Technical
Goals Committee
Policy Advisory Committee
Screening Committee
Steering Committee
Minority Participation Committees
Citizens' Committee or Association or
Special Purpose Committee
Preparative Committees
Community Council
Goals Committee
Planning Committee
Steering Committee
Review Committees
Watchdog or Review Committee
Special Purpose Committees
Citizen Association or
Special Purpose Committee
Task Performance Committees
Task Force
Work Group

The numerous citizen committees created in response to federal programs, with specific names such as Project Area Committees (PAC), Rural Area Development (RAD) committees, and Agricultural Stabilization Commission (ASC) committees, are not included in the classification. These were organized for special purposes that generally are covered by the more generic classification used above, and the purposes and structure of these federally initiated committees already have been carefully specified by the agencies responsible for their formation. The principles for general citizen committee use will be equally applicable to these special committees.

The illustrations that accompany some of the committee descriptions are of real committees that were created and conducted work sometime between 1950 and 1975. In some cases the illustration is a composite of two committees, but the account of city location, the circumstances of committee formation, strategies followed and results are essentially as they took place. Fictitious names of people have been used and communities are not identified by name or location. Accounts of unsuccessful efforts have been omitted, since the purpose is to provide illustrations of effective methods, not to document actual situations.

ADMINISTRATION COMMITTEES—
PROGRAMS AND SERVICES

Size and Composition

This is normally a relatively small committee of five to twenty persons. Special knowledge of the areas to be administered or of the constituencies to be served is an essential membership requirement. Previous program administration experience also may be desirable. The membership usually combines representatives of professionals and of "consumer" groups.

Purpose and Organizational Characteristics

As its name implies, an administrative committee is responsible for conducting a public program or service, often for a disadvantaged constituency. This type of committee may be substituted for or used in conjunction with a professional staff administrator when there is a desire for greater involvement or control by a special group than could be achieved solely through staff administration.

The committee approach has been employed in response to federal programs mandating increased minority participation in administering programs for disadvantaged groups. Health, welfare and legal services councils have been created in many communities both to plan and to carry out programs. Administration committees have proved an effective mechanism for reconciling the ideas and experience of professionals with the needs of the aggrieved groups that receive services, since representatives both of professionals and of service recipients are jointly responsible for the program. Agreement must be reached not only on program planning, but also on the allocation of substantial staff and monetary resources for which the committee may directly be responsible. In fact, the role of an administrative committee probably more nearly parallels that of a legally constituted citizen commission than any other type of citizen committee.

The membership not only may be composed of a coalition of citizen and professional groups, but it also may be a coalition of different minority segments of the community. Since there is wide variation in service requirements of different minority groups, each distinctive major group should be represented.

Some types of administrative committees may be dominated by citizen representatives, particularly those responsible for providing services at the neighborhood level. Where representation remains a true coalition of citizens representing a balance between minority and other interests in the community, the committee can function effectively, but excessive domination by a single interest group may lead to the destruction of the program itself. Where the resources at the disposal of the committee are received from outside sources who see minority control as a threat to other interests in the larger community, the tendency may be to cut off the resources. Minority control can remain only where the committee can generate its own resources or rely on those provided by friendly external sources, exemplified in some federally funded programs. Program survival in some, but certainly not all, instances may depend on maintaining a balance between members representing minority interests and those serving other special interests in the larger community.

Constituencies

The recipients of the services administered by the commission form the primary constituency of the committee. Services may be rendered to a single group or to several special interest constituencies. Each group should be separately identified to assure appropriate representation.

Resource Support Required

Since an administrative committee is responsible for programs or services, extensive resources may be needed. These may be received from local government, from state or federal funds, from the service users, or from a combination of several sources. The committee will normally hire and conduct its work through professional staff and frequently will need the full range of support required for a major public enterprise.

ADVISORY COMMITTEES—
GENERAL OR POLICY

Size and Composition

As few as nine or as many as fifty members may be used to form a general or policy advisory committee, though the number more frequently tends to be in the lower range. Persons having special knowledge of and interest in the issues under consideration should compose this committee. When a community is divided on an issue, representation from different factions should be included.

Purposes and Organizational Characteristics

This type of committee is useful in increasing the scope of citizen participation and broadening the base of community interest in programs or policy issues. It is particularly valuable when issues are either controversial or involve new areas of governmental concern. Study and advice are usually required on a single public issue or on a group of closely related public issues.

An advisory committee may be concerned with an issue on which there are divergent views and on which strongly polarized opinions have developed. A resolution of differences may be achieved by appointing leadership from different factions balanced with members who are more neutral and objective, and by charging the committee with responsibility for recommending a specific solution. The opportunity for a face-to-face discussion among those of different interests may be highly productive. The selection of a chairman who is skilled both in committee work and in conflict resolution may be a key to success.

Advisory committees are usually appointed by the mayor with the advice of the council and in consultation with any other commission or agency whom they serve. They are normally advisory to a legislative body or another official government agency or commission such as a park board, a planning commission, a housing board or a law enforcement agency. The committee usually is ad hoc, though a standing committee may occasionally be used where issues recur over a relatively long time period.

Constituencies

An advisory committee often is created by a public official to advise another group within the community. Membership usually is drawn from the leadership of those constituencies who have special interests in the public issues, and they constitute a primary constituency. Moreover, the issue may have a broad public interest orientation, making the whole community either a primary or secondary constituency. These communitywide and special interest constituencies may have differing interests, thereby creating the problem of striking a proper balance in committee representation between special and general public interests.

Resource Support Required
Support is needed from the staff serving the parent commission or agency. Public meeting rooms in public buildings can normally be used. A nominal budget may be required for investigative travel, secretarial services and publication expenses. Preparation of elaborate reports and documents would not be expected since advice on policy is required, rather than plan preparation or implementation.

•

ILLUSTRATION

General Advisory Committee

In the decade following World War II, a large southern city awoke to the problem of general economic deterioration. Unemployment was much higher than the national average; venture capital was difficult to acquire; the street and highway system and other public services needed major repairs and extensions; and the central business district contained a large inventory of obsolete buildings and inadequate parking, and had little new construction in progress. Many of the financial institutions and commercial real estate holdings were owned or controlled by two competing factions, each dominated by a forceful and aggressive business leader who retained controlling interest in a major bank. These two leaders are hereafter referred to as leader "A" and leader "B." Competition for dominant financial leadership of the community had become so intense that the two business factions not only were not cooperating, but the two leaders carefully avoided personal contact with one another, and it was rumored that they had not spoken to each other in more than three years.

The newly elected board of directors of the Chamber of Commerce discussed these economic problems at their first board meeting and agreed on the need to set aside personal animosities and work together on a broad range of programs. A strategy session was held with the mayor and it was decided that a general advisory committee should be appointed to recommend actions to be taken, both by the private and public sectors, to improve economic conditions and services in the community. While much of the work was to be advisory, some planning for policy proposals also was to be included in the charge of community responsibility.

A committee of twenty persons was appointed by the mayor, after extensive consultation with members of the city council and the Chamber of Commerce board of directors on the selection of individual members. The concensus was that the success of the committee, and indeed of the whole effort, was dependent upon obtaining the support of leader "A" and leader "B." Yet the feeling was that if "B" was asked to serve, "A" would decline a committee appointment, and vice versa. Committee membership was carefully selected from major communitywide and special interest groups, with representatives from organized labor, industry, retail business, the League of Women Voters, the local chapter of the American Institute of Architects and others, including two close associates each of "A" and "B." The mayor and the two associates of "A" together personally called upon him, outlined the purposes of the committee, and the need for his assistance. The mayor indicated names of others who were proposed for membership including leader "B." Leader "A" was not pressed for a decision but was asked to consider the matter. The mayor followed the same approach with leader "B." The associates of each leader were asked to make a follow-up call to point out that if one leader permitted the other to serve alone on such an important mission that the one who served would surely gain a dominant position in community affairs. Both "A" and "B" consented to serve.

At the first organization meeting the mayor outlined the charge of responsibility to the group who were seated around a large conference table in the municipal building. Through preplanning of the seating, "A" and "B" directly faced each other across the table. Each spoke briefly several times to the whole group, verbally sparring for a leadership role. The temporary chairman, appointed by the mayor, adroitly forced the discussion to remain issue-centered. Within twenty minutes, inadvertently and almost without being conscious of it, "A" and "B" were discussing issues with each other, rapidly defrosting their relationship. This occurred because the issues being considered were of critical importance both to the community and to each leader individually. These were issues about which neither

"A" nor "B" could remain silent. The eyeball-to-eyeball physical relationship made aloofness seem ridiculous in a public arena among one's peers, and therefore impossible to maintain. Before the end of the first session "A" and "B" were engaged in an amicable discussion of issues. In subsequent sessions, this new relationship lead to the pooling of their considerable talents and resources in charting the economic recovery of the city. Dissident factions started cooperating in strengthening social and economic institutions, expanding the economic base, and rehabilitating the city generally. There existed sufficent resources, leadership and entrepreneurial know-how within the community to plan and carry out the needed programs. The advisory committee formed the vehicle for unifying leadership for purposeful community action. It also proved useful in mobilizing private talent and resources for work on public as well as private problems. The achievements of less than ten years of effort resulted in the community becoming a model for cooperative public-private planning.

ADVISORY COMMITTEES—TECHNICAL

Size and Composition

This committee normally is composed of five to sixteen members, all of whom should have specialized expertise in the substantive area for which the committee has been assigned responsibility. Technical knowledge of the subject and willingness to provide advice are essential requirements for service. While most members should be appointed from residents of the community, a limited number of nonresidents may be used who have community ties and the needed expertise.

Purposes and Organizational Characteristics

Committee members should be capable of supplying advice and limited consultation on specific technical matters to public officials, agency staff or consultants responsible for work programs. Committee members should not be required to perform work but to review and advise responsible professionals on design and execution of technical programs. This type of guidance should improve the performance of the staff with whom the committee works. Reporting should be both to the staff and the commission or council to whom the staff is responsible. Appointment to this type of committee gives recognition to those who have unique knowledge and have earned the right to have their opinions given special consideration. This may enlist the support of specialists who might otherwise oppose or give limited support to programs. This type of committee is usually single purpose and ad hoc, and it is primarily concerned with public issues.

Constituencies

A technical advisory committee normally reports to a public legislative body or agency. Members also are accountable for the quality of their advice to their professional and technical peer groups. The primary constituencies are the recipients of the services for which the committee's technical advice is required. These may be the general public, or specific groups within the community.

Resource Support Required

Since the committee's primary responsibility is to review staff work, it will normally require no staff, budget or other resource support, except that expenses should be paid to nonresident participants who incur significant travel costs.

•

ILLUSTRATION

A Technical Advisory Committee

In the early 1950s, the city council of a large midwestern city authorized the planning agency to proceed with a study of the procedures and costs required to computerize land use data for the metropolitan area. Land use information had been previously recorded on a set of seventy-four maps, each hand-colored and mounted separately on wall panels in a special room in the planning agency offices. Planning staff members wanted to convert this information to an automatic data tabulation system that could be converted to automatic machine processing to improve the scope and rate of planning analysis, and to provide a wide range of useful information to both citizens and government officials.

Although several staff members of local banks, utility companies and a local university were skilled in automatic data processing and utilized computers for their special purposes, no staff members of the city had the ability to perform such a study. Consequently, a consulting firm was hired to conduct the study, with the stipulation that the firm work closely with the resident staff of the city. This cooperative effort was intended to provide a program that would meet the special informational needs of the community and train local staff so that they could further develop and maintain the program.

Since automatic machine processing of planning data was a relatively new type of program for which there was little previous experience or precedent in similar cities throughout the United States, city officials wanted a careful appraisal of the usefulness of the consultants' proposals, yet the city's professional staff lacked the requisite skills to make such an assessment. After discussion with the chairman of the planning commission and staff, the mayor appointed a technical advisory committee of eleven members. This committee was charged with the responsibility for reviewing the proposals of the consultants at various stages, and reporting their suggestions and recommendations to the planning staff, the consultant and the mayor.

The technical advisory committee (TAC) was composed of five members, each skilled in data processing, who were employed in private firms within the city. The remaining six members included a local economist and a local developer who were potential information users, a representative from the county assessor's office and three nonresidents. The latter were representatives of various firms manufacturing and servicing data processing machines that were being used in the community.

The committee met only four times, but in rather long sessions. The first involved an all-day session at which the research objectives and methods of the consultants' proposal were reviewed. A copy had been supplied to each member one week before the meeting. Committee members made numerous comments on the general objectives and the specific procedural approaches of the report. Criticisms were both negative and positive, but because committee members were primarily specialists, their suggestions were useful, pertinent and largely well received. Their opinions were weighed with the respect and attention due those who had already achieved professional status in the community through past performance.

Based on the responses received at the first meeting, the consultants revised the approach and conducted the study. Preliminary results were compiled and submitted to the committee for review. At this second meeting of the advisory committee, the revised draft was reviewed carefully, section by section. This second session was similar to the first and resulted in the committee giving tentative approval to the study, pending several minor modifications.

The third session occurred when the committee convened jointly with the mayor, representatives of the city council, the planning committee and city staff to review the revised preliminary draft copy of the final report of the study. In the ensuing general discussion of the proposal, the obvious knowledge and understanding of the program demonstrated by committee members was a positive influence. Citizen committee members were especially influential with elected officials who saw them in a dual role as voting citizens and as knowledgeable experts.

The final meeting of the committee occured at the call of the mayor at a special noon luncheon session, held to express official appreciation of the work of the committee. Copies of the final report were given to each committee member together with a certificate of appreciation for their work with the committee.

Several indirect benefits resulted from the work of the technical advisory committee, in addition to the more direct and obvious assistance outlined above. The advance recognition, through committee appointment, of those with special knowledge enlisted support of citizens who might otherwise have remained neutral or even have been antagonistic to the program. The prerogatives of knowledge in a community require respect and recognition. While those with special expertise should not feel that they have exclusive control of their discipline, they may rightly believe that they should be consulted on public policy issues involving their unique areas of competency. Failure to give this opportunity may alienate support and stimulate hostility among those citizens who can generate great political pressure to defeat an issue.

Another indirect result of the work of the technical advisory committee relates to the importance of informal communication channels in generating public support. The data systems vice-president (Bill Jennings) of a large local bank who served on the TAC had lunch with four business associates. When the subject of the new information system program of the city came up in general discussion, his positive response and five minute explanation of the program did more to generate support among his colleagues than could have been accomplished through a variety of more formal and costly educational approaches.

Each business associate in turn, when asked by others about the program, responded in some way as follows: "Bill Jennings has checked it out and thinks it's a good program, so it must be all right." This word of mouth approval that passes among trusted associates of the community is sure evidence of public understanding and support.

ADVISORY COMMITTEES—SCREENING

Size and Composition

A screening committee usually is relatively small in size, ranging from five to nine in number, but occasionally is somewhat larger. Membership normally is composed of representatives from several interest groups who are directly concerned with the primary purpose for which the committee is created, especially those groups whom the appointing authority feels should be brought into the decision-making process. A screening committee may be formed as a subcommittee of a larger citizens' organization or official public agency. All of the members may be selected from the parent agency and from other organizations and citizen groups who share a strong interest in the issues involved.

Purposes and Organizational Characteristics

A screening committee is a special type of advisory committee. When a careful study and selection must be made among several alternative courses of action, the use of a screening committee has several advantages. The committee is advisory in that it reviews alternatives and recommends one or more courses of action to the parent organization or group to whom it reports, but it does not actually make the selection. This "screening" process conducted by representatives from various interest groups not only increases the number of participants in the decisionmaking process, it also tends to reduce charges of partisan politics in the selection process. A city manager or a consulting firm appointed after going through the filtering of a screening committee review normally has great initial credibility because the selection process was seen as "objective." Citizens tend to view the work of the screening as curtailing the council's opportunity to make a "political appointment."

Perhaps the most commonly used type of screening committee is one appointed to interview and recommend applicants for public positions, either consultants or upper level staff, such as a city manager. The intensive investigation and interview of a large number of applicants may be more effectively conducted by a small representative group than by a legislative body or other large organizations. Choices can be reduced in number for final review and selection by the parent organization. A screening committee also may be effective in studying and recommending action where public policy or program alternatives are being considered. Usually the issues with which the committee is concerned have already been identified by other organizations, and the choices to be reviewed by the screening committee are relatively specific.

Constituencies

Three groups usually form the primary constituencies of the screening committee. These include the agency to which the committee reports, the groups from which committee membership has been drawn and the general public. Since most screening committees are concerned with major public issues, their most important constituency is the larger public whose interest they represent. Most interaction will occur between committee members and the group to whom they make recommendations, and this organization to whom they report will tend to be viewed by screening committee members as their primary constituency.

Resource Support Required

The short-term ad hoc nature of most screening committee responsibilities, and the fact that they normally are giving advice about alternatives that have been previously specified, limits the types and amount of resources required. In most instances the committee will need only a public conference room for conducting interviews and for deliberation, and the assistance of professional staff from the public agency that was involved in the initial preparation of alternatives being reviewed by the committee. Most staff input will tend to be informational rather than advisory in nature. Support staff should be present and participate only as requested by the committee.

ADVISORY COMMITTEES—STEERING

Size and Composition

The number of members of a steering committee may vary widely depending on the size of the community and the complexity of the issues with which the committee is concerned. Committee membership may range from ten to 150 and should represent a broad cross-section of community leadership and power structure. Members should be selected for their ability to influence other citizens in support of a proposed program and for their willingness to use their leadership or reputation in support of the proposal.

Purpose and Organizational Characteristics

A steering committee is used to gain public acceptance of proposed policies and to give support and guidance to bond compaigns and other policy programs, especially those requiring a referendum. Most of the members should be selected for their prominence and positions of leadership and influence in the community. A primary objective is to solidify community leadership in support of a proposal. Members do not normally become intensely involved in the work of the campaign, but their names are used for support in attendant publicity. Selected individuals may personally appear as supporting speakers at civic meetings and have spot appearances on local radio and television stations. This ad hoc committee's responsibility normally is not to make policy but to support and give visibility to proposals.

Membership should be carefully selected and contacted in advance of appointment to determine willingness to serve. The committee membership is generally appointed by the mayor with the advice of councilmen and civic leaders. An accurate and comprehensive review of the proposal and the policy issues and cost implications should be presented at the organization meeting. The early elimination of misinformation combined with peer group pressure and the prestige of being selected for a public leadership position frequently will generate support from otherwise disinterested citizens.

Steering committees have been used in goal development programs to guide or "steer" the community toward adoption or implementation of the program prepared by the goals committee. The steering committee may be actively involved in planning strategies and courses of action ranging from information and education programs for citizens and public officials to proposals for revamping the planning agency or changing the allocation of local fiscal resources to channel funds to needs identified in the goals program.

In some communities, the term "steering" has been used to describe a committee that is responsible for reviewing alternative public policies or programs and steering or advising as to the course of action that should be followed. This use of the term "steering" tends to be a misnomer since such a committee, in fact, performs a role identical to a general or policy advisory committee as described herein.

Constituencies

For a steering committee to be fully effective its membership should have representation from every major voter block within the community. Since steering committees usually are concerned with broadly based or communitywide issues, the whole community usually forms the committee's primary constituency. However, the community is an aggregation of many different interest groups. To assure the broadest possible citizen contact, minority and other special interest constituencies need to be identified, and leaders from those groups should be included in the membership of the steering committee. The primary constituencies for most members will tend to be the one or more special groups with whom the member is identified as a leader, although these special groups may, in fact, be quite secondary as constituencies.

Resource Support Required

Staff who are knowledgeable about the proposals will need to brief the committee. In a large city, the public information campaign may be run by professionals and normally will utilize membership in the roles outlined above. In smaller communities where professional staff and financing are not available for this purpose, the members of the committee often may become personally active in planning and conducting an information campaign. This latter requires budget for publicity including printing, stenographic services, and support personnel. Much work, such as telephone contacts, may be performed by volunteers. Office space outside of the city hall or other public buildings should be used. This may be either donated or rented space. Public funds should not be used to promote bond proposals or to support committees who endorse proposals.

●

ILLUSTRATION

A Steering Committee

Glancing at his watch, Jeff Marshall quickly placed the files he had been reviewing in a neat stack on his desk and strolled by the desk of

his secretary to tell her that he would not return until after lunch. He was the general manager of a family-owned department store, started by his father, that for more than forty years had occupied a prime location in the central business district of a western city of 160,000 people. Several times in recent years he had considered moving to a suburban location, but he liked the personal contact with other business and civic leaders afforded by his store location just three blocks from city hall.

The early fall morning was warm and sunny as Jeff crossed the street and stopped at a midblock men's specialty shop. The owner of the shop, Richard James, had been a lifelong friend, but Jeff had a special purpose for this midmorning visit. Long recognized as an active leader in civic affairs, he had been appointed to serve on a steering committee, created by the mayor and city council, to assist in conducting a campaign in support of a large bond issue. The bond election, to be held in less than four weeks, was called to provide monies for street and water supply improvements, flood control projects, and several new neighborhood and community parks and recreation centers. The expansion and repair of the water supply and distribution system was critically needed, and the other projects were considered to be high priority items by many people, yet the level of citizen support was difficult to measure. Although the bond program had received vigorous endorsement from the Citizens Improvement Council and had good editorial support from the local press, there was little evidence of either strong support for or opposition to the measures.

During discussions of strategy for promoting the bond issue, held by a small group of public officials and business and civic leaders, several alternatives were examined. All generally concurred on the creation of a steering committee composed of fifty to sixty persons drawn from the "influentials" of the community. Membership should represent a broad socioeconomic cross-section and all large voting blocks in the community. There was some disagreement, however, as to who should create the steering committee. Some contended that the Chamber of Commerce, the Civic Improvement Council, or some group independent of the mayor and city council should be responsible for organizing the steering committee. Many citizens might feel that public officials were biased in their support and a more "neutral" citizens' organization might have greater credibility as the organizer of a group to disseminate information about bond proposals. Several other nearby cities had successfully used this approach in recent years.

The predominate view which eventually prevailed in the strategy session, however, was that the present mayor had been reelected for a second term by an overwhelming majority. He was a strong and popular leader, and his initiative in creating the steering committee would give added weight to the importance of the bond proposal.

Richard James, better known as "Dick" to his friends, unlike Jeff, did not have a deep interest in municipal affairs. And yet, he was charming and socially prominent, and though nominally interested, was one of the "influentials" whose support would help in the passage of a bond issue.

Although Dick had received a telephone call followed by a formal written invitation to serve as a member of the steering committee, the mayor also asked Jeff to follow up by personally encouraging Dick's participation. On his way to the first briefing session of the steering committee at 10 A.M. that morning, Jeff had stopped for Dick and had arranged for lunch following the briefing to give more opportunity for discussion of the issues.

They arrived at city hall to be personally greeted by the mayor and then assemble in a tight group in the first five rows of the council room. The seating arrangement was designed for photographic coverage by the metropolitan daily. At the outset it was evident that a group picture would appear in the metropolitan edition, probably on the front page the following day, accompanied by a story describing the support and responsibilities of the steering committee in the bond election coming in the near future. Each member had to be willing to have his or her prestige "used" for public endorsement of the bond proposal. More than nominal support was necessary because each member immediately realized the necessity for acquiring as many facts as possible about each proposal. It wasn't that members would be asked to fill speaking engagements of public appearances. These major public presentations would be handled by professional staff, but each steering committee member would need to respond knowledgeably in informal discussions with friends and associates who looked to them for leadership on civic affairs. Each was therefore eagerly attentive at the briefing session which was expertly handled by professional planning staff using graphic illustrations, charts and slides. A well-prepared brochure describing all proposed projects and cost estimates was given to each committee member. While the special projects staff of the planning department had prepared the large-scale information charts and statistics used in the graphic presentation, the Chamber of Commerce financed the printing of several thousand copies of the brochure. Although it was largely informational in nature, the bond proposals were clearly portrayed in the most favorable possible manner, and opponents of the proposal might rightfully object to the use of public funds for a "promotional brochure."

Numerous questions and general discussion followed the initial presentation. The rising level of enthusiasm for the package of bond projects was evident as complete but concise answers were provided to numerous questions. Each steering committee member was given several copies of the brochure for personal distribution. Also supplied were staff names and telephone numbers where answers could be quickly provided to questions that might arise during the ensuing weeks. Moreover, members were assured that their names would not be used in advertisements or other promotional material without their consent. Each participant was asked to report any strong pockets of opposition that were detected, especially if they seemed to be the result of misinformation.

Three additional members joined Jeff and Dick for lunch. Other members departed from the briefing in groups of two or more. The strongly committed and enthusiastic members reinforced and catalyzed the more reluctant participants, thereby creating a favorable political climate at the highest levels of community leadership that would filter outward, largely through an informal conversation net, to many different constituencies.

Through the mechanism of the steering committee many community leaders were forced to become knowledgeable about a public program because they were officially and publicly involved. This approach can be highly effective in implementing well-conceived public programs, but would also tend to quickly illuminate the flaws in a poorly prepared plan. The enthusiasm that was generated within the steering committee, which spread infectiously throughout the community, occurred because the bond proposals were well presented at the briefing session and were perceived as highly desirable by a large majority of the committee membership. If either the briefing or the proposals themselves were poorly prepared, support for the projects might rapidly disappear.

Most of the effective work of the steering committee occurred as members individually conversed with friends and associates and permitted their names to be used in published statements of endorsement. A few presented information to civic clubs in which they were active members. The steering committee actually met in formal sessions twice following the initial organization and briefing session. At these two sessions, staff members gave a progress report on the promotional program. Most of the time was spent in obtaining advice on certain tactics and strategy to be used in the final days of the campaign, and in staff response to questions of individual members.

All of the bond issues were approved. The smallest majority was for the flood control program which received 68 percent of all votes cast. The work of the steering committee was formally concluded when the mayor sent each member a letter on behalf of the council expressing appreciation for their efforts.

Members of this particular steering committee were not strongly active in "guiding" or "steering" the bond campaign. Professional staff largely directed the program. Steering committees responsible for guiding the adoption of policy, or directing bond campaigns where professional staff is not available, often may be much more directly involved in mapping strategies and taking personal responsibility for educating the electorate and promoting a policy or program.

MINORITY PARTICIPATION COMMITTEES

Size and Composition

Composed of nine to twenty-four persons, members are selected to assure minority representation from groups who tend to lack political power and representation in the normal channels of local government. Selection may be by election from minority interest groups, by ex officio membership or appointment from minority organizations, or by appointment by an elected local government official. Representation tends to have greater legitimacy when the selection process is controlled entirely by the minorities being represented. Some difficulty may be encountered in identifying minority organizations and appropriate selection procedures that are truly representative of minority communities and special interest groups.[1]

Purpose and Organizational Characteristics

Created as a response to federal program and funding requirements, this type of committee is intended to increase minority citizen involvement in planning, implementing and operating local urban renewal, economic and social welfare programs, frequently at the neighborhood level. A minority participation committee is similar to a special purpose committee in that special or limited interests, rather than communitywide interests, are involved. While minority participation is a primary organizational objective, this is clearly a dual purpose committee that may exercise operational responsibility for planning, advising on or administering a particular program. It is distinguished from other types of committees because it is expressly created to increase minority participation. All or a significant portion of the committee membership is exclusively from minority groups, and the selection of minority representatives is controlled by minority constituencies. Project area committees and tenant councils, required under federal urban renewal and public housing programs, are illustrations of this type of committee, as are health services councils and community action committees that may exercise policy control over specific programs.

Constituencies

The primary constituencies of minority participation committees are dependent upon the operational responsibilities of the committee, but they normally constitute two groups. The minority group or agency from which a member is elected or appointed is the most evident constituency, but all recipients of the services or policies for which the committee has direct or advisory responsibilities also are primary constituents. Where a committee is formed as a coalition of several different ethnic or racial minorities, the differing needs of these separate minority constituencies should be identified and reflected in the programs for which the committee is responsible.

Resource Support Required

Unlike other citizen committees, which normally serve without pay, a stipend and expense allowance may be needed to make possible participation of representatives from low income minorities. Some programs stipulate that stipends be provided only to members requesting funds. This selective payment or request tends to infer a declaration of poverty and will cause many members to refuse remuneration who may be in substantial need of assistance. Suitable stipends and expenses should be uniformally provided all members when large time commitments of a continuous nature are required and membership includes representatives from low income groups. Payment is not normally necessary for short-term ad hoc committee assignments. Since many of the programs for which minority committees are responsible are relatively complex, professional assistance may be required from public agency staff with the necessary expertise. In fact, a training program for all committee members may be needed to orient individuals to consumer demands and program responsibilities. Citizen committee work has proved a useful device for leadership training of minority participants, but the opportunity to interact with and have the counsel of competent, sensitive professionals may be necessary for effective committee performance where direct program and policy responsibilities are involved.

All meetings should be held in public conference rooms and located as near as possible to the place of residence or employment of the majority of minority members. In some cases, transportation may need to be provided for individual committee members who lack access to mass or personal transportation. Insofar as possible, the deliberations of committees concerned with minority interests should be held in locations centrally situated in the neighborhoods or areas where the minority constituencies reside and should be as accessible and visible as possible to those constituencies. Traveling about and being physically present in the community of concern will aid in keeping the committee members sensitive to their major responsibilities. Where policy issues are involved, committees may need to report to and receive feedback from constituencies for guidance.[2] The time, location and procedures for conducting meetings should provide an openness and accessibility for citizens who are to be the beneficiaries of committee efforts. A minority participation committee is exemplified in the illustration of the citizens association on page 71.

COMMUNITY COUNCILS OR CITIZEN COUNCILS (Mayor Initiated or Privately Initiated)

Size and Composition

Composed of forty to 300 citizens of the community, this committee should have representation from a broad socioeconomic spectrum. Membership should cover a wide range of interests, ages, employment sectors, ethnic groups and knowledge areas of the community. Many ex officio members may be appointed from existing public, private and quasi-public organizations. While members from adult middle class groups seem to predominate on most community councils, representation from youth organizations, the elderly and lower socioeconomic sectors is highly desirable.

Purposes and Organizational Characteristics

A large broadly representative citizen council normally is responsible for studying and pressing for action on a wide variety of public policies and programs. It frequently is used to study and recommend measures to overcome economic or social lethargy in the community. The council, because of its large size, usually is divided into functional area subcommittees for in-depth study of problems, with findings reported to and acted upon by the whole council. Issues on which the council develops a consensus usually result in recommendations to appropriate governmental bodies, such as support for bond issues or other public policy measures. Community council actions often result in the creation of additional organizations for direct action. It is primarily oriented to study and to catalyze action in other community organizations, rather than to directly plan specific programs. The council provides an effective mechanism for educating citizens about community problems, increasing contact with the grass roots and uniting important segments of the community in support of particular projects. This is usually a standing committee that is concerned with broad public interest rather than limited special interest or private interest issues.

The privately initiated citizen council varies slightly from a mayor-appointed council in that it develops its own by-laws, has a greater ex officio membership drawn from other community organizations and therefore may be somewhat more broadly representative and have greater continuity of operation. It may also be more actively involved in the actual planning and promoting of projects and issues and tends to be less dominated by local government issues than a mayor-initiated council. Sample bylaws for a privately created citizen council are given in Appendix B.

Constituencies

The wide representation of the council members clearly dictates that the community as a whole is the primary constituency, as the council's name implies. Individual representatives who are elected or serve in an ex officio capacity from an interest group or organization, however, may view their parent organization as their primary constituency. Their initial motive for participation may reflect a concern that their interest group be represented in the affairs of the community council; and this desire to exert influence on public policy through council activities may be a continuing purpose of many members, particularly those from minorities. This expansion of citizen access to public policy issues can be an important function of the council, thereby providing opportunities for leadership training and opening new channels of communication to grassroots constituencies who may have had no previous direct contact with the policy processes of local government.

Resource Support Required

This council must have the support of technical staff, which is frequently borrowed from public agencies. A mayor-initiated council will tend to have greater access to and support of city planning staff. Privately initiated councils may have a small, independent, paid staff financed by contributions, but most information must be supplied by volunteer efforts of the membership or by technical staff from public agencies or private corporations. Funds for secretarial services and limited publication of reports are needed. Public conference rooms can be utilized for study and general sessions.

●

ILLUSTRATION

Community Council

A southwestern city with a population of 90,000 within the corporate limits and an additional 35,000 people in suburban areas faced severe economic problems with the announced closing of a major federal airforce installation. A general disspiritedness and lethargy seemed to permeate city government and other civic affairs. Land use patterns were shifting as new suburban housing and shopping centers increased the economic stresses in the central business district. Competition among local developers and banking institutions increased, and feelings of anger and frustration replaced the spirit of enthusiasm and cooperation that was evident during previous periods of the community's history.

A new mayor was elected on the promise that he would get the city moving again. One of his first acts was to create a citizen council composed of 100 citizens. The mayor's staff identified about thirty-five major civic organizations in the community from which the council members were drawn. Included on the list were several major civic clubs, such as the Lions, Rotarians and Kiwanians; the League of Women Voters; the P.T.A.; garden clubs; the Chamber of Commerce; the student senates of the two highschools; professional women's organizations; local chapters of the American Institute of Architects, American Society of Civil Engineers and the Bar Association; and other similar groups. A letter, over the mayor's signature, was mailed to each of these organizations explaining the purpose of the new citizen council and requesting that the names of two nominees willing to work on the council be submitted from each group. Each elected council member was asked to submit three nominations, and the mayor made ten additional appointments to assure representation from youth groups, the elderly and several minority racial organizations.

The organization meeting was held at a special 7:00 A.M. breakfast during the first week in May. The breakfast hour was selected because it was different from the more traditional evening dinner, and in the mayor's words, "symbolically expresses the shared experience of breaking bread together, then going out to the work of the day." The 7:00 A.M. hour also involved a minimum of time conflicts for the highly diverse participants; and the cost of breakfast, which was paid from the mayor's expense account, was much less than an evening dinner.

The mayor explained the purpose of the council and presented a written copy of the charge of responsibility to each member. Temporary officers were elected including a chairperson, vice-chairperson and a recorder. A member of the special projects division of the city planning department was assigned to work with the citizen council. Other professional staff from city departments were to be available on request.

The council selected a committee to prepare bylaws and recommendations on council organization. This study resulted in the division of the council into a series of study area subcommittees: economic development, technical education, community arts and aesthetics, community recreation, transportation, social services and resources, the natural environment, general government and finance, and law enforcement. A chairperson was elected for each work area, and all members were assigned to one or more subcommittee on the basis of their personal preferences, and their interests and abilities. As subcommittee studies progressed, additional subcommittees were created to study special problems such as street improvements, open space planning and preservation, housing for the elderly, industrial development, solid waste management and others. New subcommittees were established when a need became apparent.

Each subcommittee was responsible for making a study of the assigned area of concern and reporting findings to the whole council. Following a subcommittee report, the council could adopt the recommendations, ask for further study or initiate measures to implement the proposal.

The effectiveness of the council work rested on several factors. The careful study of public issues by a large group of interested citizens often generated new ideas and certainly broadened the support base for action. Community confidence and enthusiasm was infectious and tended to displace lethargy and general despair. The citizen council was primarily a study and action recommending group. New policies and programs which the citizen council developed were recommended to the city council, the school board, the Chamber of Commerce and other official civic agencies. On their own initiative, the council at times found it necessary to work for the creation of a new agency such as an industrial foundation or an environmental board.

The council described here was officially created in 1953 and after more than twenty years of continuous operation is still an active force in community affairs. Its influence developed slowly and it was most effective in creating a new avenue of citizen participation, education and leadership training. Many elected political leaders and members of official boards and commissions received their first public service experience by appointment to the citizen council.

GOALS COMMITTEES

Size and Composition

A goals committee membership may range from fifteen to fifty or more in number; however, it is not unusual to create a central coordination committee or an executive committee of ten to thirty-five and a series of subcommittees having specific substantive areas of responsibility for goal development. Several hundred citizens may actively participate in subcommittee work focused on such areas as employment, housing, health, education, transportation, law enforcement and environmental quality. The membership of the central committee should be representative of major social, economic and physical environmental interests of the community. Subcommittee members should have special interest in and particular knowledge of the substantive issues with which they are involved.

Purpose and Organization

A goals committee has many of the same characteristics as a policy advisory committee, but with some significant differences. The citizen goals committee may be advisory to an official planning agency or city council, or it may be charged with responsibility for the actual preparation of goals. Since its primary purpose is to aid in the development and appraisal of community goals, it must be concerned with a whole range of economic issues, social services and environmental factors, all of which affect the quality of life in the community.

Goals committees may be standing or ad hoc, but in either case, the efforts usually require two or more years of intensive effort, extensive communication with individual citizens and special interest groups, and modification and updating of the results of initial efforts. Community goals tend to become rapidly outdated, either because they are realized or because they become obsolete. The goal-making and evaluation process, therefore, should be relatively continuous.

There seems to be an increasing tendency to organize an independent goal preparative committee to supplement official agency work. This trend is illustrated by the organization of the goals committee of the city of Cupertino, California. The mayor appointed a representative group of citizens in 1970 "to establish long range community goals prior to the adoption of a new General Plan." The mayor stated that

> the council purposely maintained a "hands-off" attitude, to insure that the results would be a free expression of the community's wishes. Therefore, the committee determined its own areas of interest and established its own ground rules for data gathering and research, deliberation, goal formulation, adoption and implementation, drawing on the resources of city staff as necessary.

The citizen study in Cupertino consisted of several phases. A small representative group of citizens held discussions and "brainstorming" sessions during the initial phase that focused on the identification of issues. The number of committee participants then was greatly expanded and divided into functional subcommittees: government methods, community services, physical community development, housing and public finance. Months of subcommittee studies and debate resulted in a comprehensive goals and policies plan that was ratified by the entire goals committee. The final phase resulted in the program being turned over to a citizen steering committee to guide the adoption and implementation of goals through official government action.[3]

The committee approach used in Cupertino is representative of goals programs of other cities throughout the United States. Citizens of Los Angeles used a similar process in the mid-1960s, and a parallel effort is currently in progress in Corpus Christi, Texas.[4]

Constituencies

The primary constituencies of a goals committee are difficult to identify since each citizen and organized group within the community is directly affected by the allocation of public resources that is an inherent part of any priority system of goals. The goals committee probably should have the most diverse possible constituency. Not only does a comprehensive goals program need to include broad elements such as mass transit, health services and regional recreation facilities that benefit most citizens of the community, but it also should be directed toward the special needs of low visibility and less politically powerful constituencies such as the poor, the elderly, the very young and disadvantaged ethnic minorities. The goals program, which forms the basis for a comprehensive community plan, will need to cover both narrow and minute segments of community interests as well as large constituencies.

Resource Support Required

Staff support is the most vital resource required for effective performance by a goals committee. Since information and study are required in many different areas of concern, assistance is needed from staff skilled in comprehensive planning methods. Both resident planning staff and consultants may be used, and help frequently may need to be obtained from professionals in community renewal, health, education, social services and other areas requiring specialized expertise. Seldom will the citizen volunteer efforts of a goals committee prove effective unless supplemented with knowledgeable staff support. Office space, clerical staff and library resources are needed. Some travel and other expenses may be incurred, with the amount of the required budget contingent on the size of the community and the complexity of the issues involved.

●

ILLUSTRATION

Goals Committee

Five women sat around the table in thoughtful conversation. They had gathered earlier in the den of Ellen Clark's home for a league committee meeting. All had been local residents of this city of 34,000 for several years, were active members of the League of Women Voters and frequently participated in civic affairs. Having concluded their committee business, they lapsed into a discussion of the need for more sidewalks leading to elementary schools and the traffic hazards confronting children generally throughout the city. Kris Kay, the mother of two children, ages eight and eleven, observed that no real thought was given to the design of the city for children. "In fact," she commented, "I have attended both city council and planning commission meetings several times a year since we moved here nine years ago, and I don't remember a single discussion before either public body that dealt with the issue of children's needs in planning this city. Occasionally someone might bring up the need for better signs at school crossings," she continued, "but I am talking about really giving some thought to planning a safe, interesting and even exciting environment for children, not only around the home, but in other parts of the city as well. Generally, the adult with an automobile seems to have it best. It is difficult to find a safe place to walk or ride a bicycle."

Immediately the conversation became more animated. Mary Rogers commented, "I wonder how priorities for development are set up in the first place. It seems to me that the council deals with problems when a person or a group complains about something, but there must be lots of things that don't get tended to because neither the mayor nor the council sees them as problems." "I remember several years ago," Ellen responded, "that a consultant was hired to prepare a plan for the city, but I don't think anything was said about goals or priorities. I wonder how they decided what to plan?"

This conversation continued for some time and then abruptly terminated when Debora May suggested, "Why don't we ask the mayor to a league meeting to discuss these same questions?" All concurred that it was a good idea, and Debora agreed to discuss it with the league president.

The mayor did speak to the league. He responded candidly to most questions, but artfully evaded a direct answer when asked how the goals of the community were established. Several women pressed the issue and he reacted with a brief discussion of the annual budget-making process, but this obviously did not satisfy most of the group.

Not letting the issue drop, they appointed a small study committee to look into the matter of community goals. In the process of this study they contacted the officials of several cities. While most communities seemed to follow the traditional approach of reacting to problems as they became evident, several officials indicated that their comprehensive plan contained both general goals and specific objectives. The mayor of one large city outlined the procedures followed in the goals study used in the development of their current comprehensive plan. Several members of the study committee decided to propose a similar program for use in developing goals and development concepts and setting priorities for their community. Although the league did not officially endorse or sponsor the effort, numerous informal discussions ensued between members of the study committee and various city officials. Finally, the mayor and council agreed to follow through on the proposal drafted by the study committee to formulate goals for the community.

Central to the effort was the creation of a Citizen Committee on Community Goals and Priorities of about forty members. It was locally known as the CGP committee, and had representation from major interest groups within the community. In addition, two members were to be selected from each of several city boards and councils including the city council, planning commission, park and recreation board, environmental board, health council, human relations commission and the school board. Civic clubs, labor unions, the Chamber of Commerce, the parent-teachers association and similar groups were asked to select members, and the highschool student council was asked to select five representatives.

Arrangements were made for a one day retreat to be held on the campus of the state university located sixty miles away. Faculty members from the departments of sociology, philosophy, political science and economics agreed to serve as resource people, and the session was to be coordinated by the director of the university's Institute of Community Development. Expenses of participants and the costs of resource personnel were paid out of a $5,600 budget. A breakdown showed $4,000 from a city council appropriation and $1,600 from private sources.

The coordinator opened with a brief presentation on quality of life factors and measurements, followed by a brain-storming session on personal perceptions of what constituted quality of life. Then, general discussion ensued including responses from faculty resource people.

Immediately following lunch the group was divided into five sub-committees under the following main headings: economic environment, political environment, physical environment, social environment and health environment. For the next two hours, under the guidance of a faculty resource person, each committee discussed the quality of life implications for their subject area. First, they dealt with national, then with state and finally with local level issues. After reassembly, each group presented a short summary report of their deliberations and conclusions. The session terminated with a discussion of how quality of life measurements could be used in the development of their city.

The campus setting, away from telephones and the busy routine of daily life, was ideal for the retreat. As their community became temporarily more remote, it could also be viewed somewhat more objectively, and each person could give at least one full day of uninterrupted thought and attention to its problems.

Following the retreat the CGP committee membership was divided into ten subcommittees, as follows:

1. Housing and residential neighborhoods
2. Employment and the economy
3. Education
4. Recreation, parks, open space and aesthetic quality
5. Law enforcement
6. Transportation and communication
7. Environmental conservation and pollution abatement

8. The quality of community life and social values
9. Comprehensive planning and citizen involvement
10. Human rights and the special needs of the aged, ethnic and racial minorities, and children

Subcommittees were assigned responsibility for studying and developing community goals for their topic areas. Each was instructed to give special consideration to the needs of preschool children, those in the six to thirteen and fourteen to nineteen age groups, and the elderly. They were also advised by the chairman to coordinate this facet of their study with the human rights subcommittee.

All members of the CGP committee were assigned, on the basis of personal choice, to either one or two subcommittees. Moreover, the membership of each subcommittee was expanded to include others from the community who had either special interest or expertise in the subject area. Most of the work of goal development was conducted at the subcommittee level by the members themselves in consultation with city staff and advisors from the state university. Once every two months a general meeting was held of all CGP committee members, including all new members added to the subcommittees, to receive reports on the progress of different subcommittees.

As an aid in determining citizen perceptions of their community and what they would like it to be, a social statistics class from the state university prepared and administered a survey of citizen opinion during the third month of the study, and the results were given to all CGP members.[5]

Because the city was relatively small, most subcommittees were able to complete their studies and submit preliminary written reports in twelve to eighteen months. Following completion of its study, each subcommittee selected one member to serve on an executive committee to coordinate the different reports and prepare a final goals program report. The chairman and vice-chairman of the CGP committee served in the same roles on the twelve member executive committee. City planning staff provided writing and research support skills to the executive committee. The task of preparing the final report required approximately ten months.

During the period of the subcommittee studies and the preparation of the full report by the executive committee the desirability of public hearings was discussed. Staff members stated that, especially in larger cities, feedback from public hearings was an important aspect of the goal development process. The CGP committee decided to prepare its initial report without hearings, however, and then urge the city council to hold hearings on the committee recommendations. Even though this procedure probably would require some revisions in the committee's recommendations, CGP members felt that if public hearings were the responsibility of public officials they would more directly share in the goal development effort.

The goals program report, as prepared by the executive committee, was approved by the CGP membership, with some minor amendments, and submitted to the mayor approximately twenty-eight months after the initial organization meeting of the committee.[6] Following the adoption of the goals program report, the last act of the committee was to select from its membership twelve persons to serve on a steering committee to guide the review and adoption of the report through the planning commission and the city council. Its work completed, each member went on to other community tasks, but with considerable new insight about the city in which they lived and the problems connected with the allocation of its public resources among many different constituencies.

CITIZEN PLANNING COMMITTEES (PUBLIC AGENCY OR PRIVATELY INITIATED)

Size and Composition

A planning committee usually is composed of seven to twenty-four persons, but planning associations formed by citizens in a large metropolitan area may have 100 or more members. Persons are normally appointed for membership based on two characteristics. Each member should have substantive knowledge of the area for which the committee has planning responsibility or capacity for leadership in the issues of concern.

Purposes and Organizational Characteristics

The purpose of a planning committee is precisely what the name implies: It is to plan something. The scale and complexity of planning responsibility varies widely. Publically created planning committees usually differ substantially from privately initiated committees.

Committees of public origin usually are created to prepare plans for public programs that are relatively controversial or that involve an area of concern for which no existing governmental agency has responsibility, or to deal with a public issue of interest only to a small segment of the total population of the community. A planning committee is a useful device for resolving differences among factions in the community by bringing together leaders from different factions and charging them with responsibility for devising a solution. New areas of public concern frequently are made the responsibility of a citizen planning committee until desirable operational patterns can be established. Any lack of success of an ad hoc citizen planning committee normally will be subject to far less public criticism than would result from a similar failure by an official government agency. Use of a citizen planning committee is also an effective way to limit public agency or governmental responsibility in areas of special interest to a limited number of citizens.

To illustrate, a small delegation of drag-racing enthusiasts asked the city council of a midwestern city to build a strip for racing. The council established a citizen planning committee to make preliminary plans for the location, type of track, spectator and service facilities required, and to investigate means of financing the project. This approach was politically acceptable in that it permitted a full study of the issues without committing public resources, and it utilized citizens with special knowledge and interest in the project. At the same time, by appointing a "public" committee, the issues were open to public scrutiny so that they could be debated by all interested citizens within the community.

Privately created citizen committees or associations tend to have broader and more complex missions, since they are frequently used as a substitute for or a supplement to official local government planning agencies. Well known examples include the Regional Plan Association of New York and the Greater Baltimore Committee, Inc.[7] Created by the initiative of local civil leaders, these committees engage in planning specific projects and in areawide comprehensive planning, when governmental planning agencies are thought to be inadequate.

Some planning committees have resulted from frustrations of neighborhood groups who feel that official planning efforts do not reflect their interests. Since these groups tend to be special interest oriented and carry on activities other than planning, they are discussed under the heading, "Citizen Associations."

Constituencies

Citizen planning committees normally have two groups of constituents. The first are those who will be directly affected by the programs of projects being planned. These recipients of the planning effort form the primary constituency; however, many other groups or the community as a whole may also be parties of interest and therefore form either primary or secondary constituencies.

Resource Support Required

Professional staff with planning expertise in the areas of concern will be needed. Staff support may come from existing official planning agencies for publically created planning committees. Privately organized committees may borrow public agency staff, but usually will hire their own consultants or full-time personnel. These normally are financed through private contributions, subscriptions and grants. An independent staff is essential when private planning groups desire programs that differ from official proposals. Sufficient funding will be needed for staff, office space, equipment and other operational expenses. Whether this is supplied from private or public sources will depend upon the function of the committee.

●

ILLUSTRATION

Planning Committee

For several years, the city council of a southwestern city of 60,000 people had, with no apparent success, attempted to gain community support for the construction of a civic center, including a new city hall. The dilapidated state of existing public buildings attested to the need for new facilities. In the words of one councilman, "How can we continue to file condemnation suits against buildings that are substantially better than our city hall?" The lack of action was not primarily due to public apathy, but seemed to result from disagreement among three factions about where a civic center should be located. Several widely scattered sites had been suggested, and each faction lobbied for a different location. The impasse continued for more than a decade, during the tenure of three different mayors.

A newly elected mayor, early in his first year of office, appointed sixteen citizens to serve as a civic center planning committee. Careful attention was given to the selection of committee members, and as it turned out, this was essential to the success of the mission. A distinguished business and civic leader, not previously identified with any faction, was appointed as temporary chariman and later was elected by the committee members to serve as permanent chairman. The principal leader of each of the three factions was appointed to the committee as well as an additional supporter of each faction. The remaining nine members were appointed from relatively diverse community groups. The committee was composed of ten men and six women, ranging in age from twenty-three to sixty-four, all with a record of civic activity in the community. Approximately half of the membership had a neutral position on the civic center issue, though none were in opposition to the proposal. To provide professional assistance, three members of the local planning department staff were assigned to conduct research work for the committee. The staff skills included architecture, central business district planning, general land use planning and fiscal policies planning.

The first two meetings of the committee were devoted to general discussions of the need for civic center development and the best approaches for studying the problem. The committee agreed to break into three subcommittees, one to study what elements should be included in a civic center, the second to review and evaluate alternative locations, and the third to analyze different financing possibilities.

Professional staff prepared detailed reports for each subcommittee and obtained additional information as requested. Civic center plans were acquired from other cities of comparable size, and visits were made by committee members to four cities that were reputed to have good facilities. Reports of each subcommittee were prepared and submitted to the whole committee.

The civic center composition subcommittee reported first, outlining the things that might be appropriate for inclusion in a civic center and giving the advantages and disadvantages of centralized and decentralized development. The elements considered were a municipal building housing management, legislative and law enforcement functions; a central library; a general purpose community social and craft center, including facilities for both youth and the elderly; a recreation center with swimming pools and gymnasium; a central

U.S. Post Office; and general office space for public utilities. Following much discussion, a strong consensus developed among committee members to include all but the recreation center and the general office space in a single unified civic center development.

The location subcommittee was concerned with the most controversial issue, but after agreement was reached on what elements should be contained in a civic center, the number of alternatives as to location were substantially reduced. It was evident that several sites previously proposed by different factions were too small. Four alternatives for sites were studied, and preliminary estimates of acquisition costs, transportation access and other factors were compiled and evaluated by professional staff.

In the early stages of the study, representatives of different factions strongly defended their earlier proposals, but as study and discussion continued in a series of meetings spanning several months, the inadequacies of some of the former proposals became apparent. Two factors contributed to defining an acceptable course of action. First, the carefully prepared studies of competent professionals broadened the scope of the project and gave new information on the problems and the alternatives available for consideration. Second, the discussion of each issue occurred among a fairly large group of interested, relatively objective citizens. Members with previously developed biases had to defend their viewpoints from a minority position. The proponent for each faction was in a forum without the emotional support of other members of the faction, where reason and logic were necessary to generate communitywide rather than special interest support. Each proponent had to justify a position to opposition leaders face-to-face, with the more "neutral" committee members serving as the final judges, since their supporting votes would be required.

The committee finally recommended a civic center site that had not been previously considered by any faction. The site chosen was much larger than anything formerly anticipated. The committee recommendations were presented in a comprehensive report (prepared by professional staff) that carefully outlined the alternative possibilities that had been considered and the factors supporting the final recommendations on civic center composition, location and financing.

The city council adopted the committee recommendations and, after wide dissemination of the committee study including review and approval by the city planning commission, a referendum on a bond issue was called to fund land acquisition and the first phase of construction. The issue passed with 68 percent of the ballots cast in support of the issue.

REVIEW AND WATCHDOG COMMITTEES

Size and Composition

A relatively small committee normally ranging from five to fifteen persons, the membership of a review committee usually is appointed from those who have special knowledge of the issues involved. Since these committees may be created at the insistence of dissident groups, the membership should contain citizens with strong interests in the issues with which the committee is concerned. Some members may be openly skeptical or highly critical of the programs that they are monitoring. A watchdog committee composed entirely of "friendly" citizens will largely negate the committee's effectiveness in carrying out the review and monitoring purposes for which it was created.

Purpose and Organizational Characteristics

These committees are usually created to review the actions of public officials or agencies or areas of social or economic inequities. Watchdog committees composed of representatives from highly critical factions of the community may be used to monitor fiscal policy, budget-making or the expenditure of capital improvement funds. The close review of official actions often provides committee members, and the constituencies to whom they report, with new insights into the complexities of financing governmental programs and implementing public policies. Citizen review will also tend to increase the accountability of public officials and the care given to the expenditure of public funds.

Review committees also may be used to study and report on situations of racial discrimination and other areas of social or economic injustices. Committees on fair housing practices, fair employment practices and environmental pollution have been used to identify and focus public attention on special problem areas.

Watchdog committees are usually ad hoc, appointed by a mayor or a government official in response to pressure of a group of concerned citizens or established by a citizens' organization. The problems that these committees identify and review eventually may be made the responsibility of a government agency or a legally created standing committee such as a planning commission or a human relations commission.

Constituencies

The primary constituencies of most watchdog committees are the dissident groups responsible for the creation of the committee, or the recipients of public services being reviewed by the committee. In some cases, irate taxpayers may create a watchdog committee to monitor government expenditures. The taxpayers comprising the group that formed the committee form the primary constituency. In other instances citizens, outraged by discriminating practices, may force the city council to create a committee to review actions that impinge on individual freedoms guaranteed by federal and state constitutions. Citizens whose freedom from discrimination is being protected are a primary constituency, as are those causing the formation of the committee. To be sure, the public as a whole also may benefit from close committee scrutiny of public actions and thereby be either a primary or secondary constituency, but benefits seldom will be equally distributed to all citizens. Those most affected by those factors that were the initial cause for concern usually will comprise the primary constituency.

Resource Support Required

The members of these committees usually will have the competency and interest to personally conduct most of their own studies and reviews of issues with which they are concerned. They may need a limited amount of technical assistance drawn either from independent sources or from public agencies. Some funds for secretarial and publication and office expenses may be necessary. The amount of budget required will be dependent upon the nature and scope of the studies covering the issues involved.

SPECIAL PURPOSE COMMITTEES OR CITIZEN ASSOCIATIONS

Size and Composition

Composed of nine to fifty or more members, the size of the committee normally will be determined by the issues and the size of the interest group that forms the committee. Members are elected or appointed from one or more groups having common concerns and problems, and who have special interest in the issues involved. The committee may be a coalition representing several different interest groups, such as a central business district association, or it may be formed to deal with the problems of a single neighborhood, as exemplified by a project area committee formed under urban renewal.

Purpose and Organizational Characteristics

Constituted from individuals and groups with common interests who organize to achieve a special purpose, this type of committee may focus upon a public issue having limited territorial concern, upon a special function, or upon a largely private or highly local public issue that has been neglected or ignored by existing government agencies. Frequently created by citizen initiative, the committee may succeed in making the issue a governmental one or in channeling a larger share of public resources to constituency interests. While special purpose committees tend to be self-serving, the issues on which they focus may be of broad public concern. Planning and action programs normally are an important part of the committee's work effort.

Special purpose committees take a variety of forms including neighborhood associations; project area committees (PAC) under urban renewal; central business district associations; industrial, economic and area development commissions; and community action program (CAP) committees for target neighborhoods under model cities. These committees, generated either by an interest group or by a government agency, may be ad hoc or standing. Special purpose committees created to comply with federal requirements for funding under urban renewal, model cities, community development and other similar programs have responsibilities similar to those outlined in this section or to those identified for minority participation committees.

Constituencies

Special purpose committees normally have one or more special interest groups as a primary constituency. Many committee members may participate almost solely to further their own personal interests, while others may represent a much larger citizens' group. Most members will tend to view a special group, rather than the larger community, as their primary constituency. This will be a dominant tendency whether the committee is privately created or is formed in response to federal program requirements.

Resource Support Required

Privately created committees usually need staff assistance supplied by donations of time and money from private sources. Committees serving under government agency auspices should be provided budget and staff support from public sources. Unlike most other committees, meetings may be held in private facilities and may be conducted privately. Private space for committee work may be needed. The use of public space and other public resources, in many cases, may be inappropriate when the special interests of a particular group are being pursued.

●

ILLUSTRATION

Citizens Association
(Project Area Committee)

The city council of a large southwestern city designated a 1,250 acre mixed use district as an urban renewal project area. Commercial and industrial uses were interspersed throughout residential neighborhoods. While black occupancy of housing and commercial buildings predominated, whites also lived and worked within the area. The renewal plan, prepared by consultants working under contract for the urban renewal agency, proposed large areas for clearance and conversion to public housing. Extensive rehabilitation measures were designated for other portions of the project area.

In the early stages of the project, a citizen advisory committee was appointed by the city council to review proposed plans and advise agency staff. As relocation started, prior to demolition of the first residential and commercial structures, the distrust and resistance of project area residents intensified. The political power of the several thousand occupants of this large urban renewal district could not be ignored and, as a result, the city council, urban renewal agency and local HUD officials, in consultation with citizen leaders, agreed to reconstitute the advisory committee to broaden participation and give project area citizens full control of committee representation.

Membership selection was by election, conducted by representatives from community organizations existing in the area in accordance with guidelines established through a consultation of various interested parties. Included in this group on election procedures were local representatives from the federal Department of Housing and Urban Development (HUD), the local urban renewal agency and three social service committees that existed in the project area.

For purposes of voting, the project area was divided into three districts and one polling place was established near the center of each. The election was publicized extensively, using local newspapers, radio and television, and staff were available at each polling place to explain purposes and procedures to interested citizens. Those eligible to run for committee membership and to vote included all owners and renters of property and all operators of businesses in the project area. On a date publically advertised, twenty-nine members were elected to serve staggered three year terms on the new project area committee (PAC).

While the initial purpose of PAC was to advise the urban renewal agency on the planning and execution of the renewal program, the committee also exercised minority participation, watchdog and preparative roles. These different committee activities were determined, to a large extent, by the individual concerns of committee members. The motivation for participation by most PAC members stemmed from vested interests. Members were either owners of property to be relocated or operators of businesses in the area. Having observed the difficulties of neighbors in similar situations, they were seeking ways to protect their own interests through increased knowledge and political organization.

For many, PAC membership was the first chance to be involved in public policy decisions that drastically affected their lives. This was a new and demanding task for which they were ill-equipped. The first two weeks of committee work were devoted to nightly training sessions with technical staff. The major requirements of the 1954 Federal Housing Act were outlined and plans for renewal of the project area were discussed.

At the outset, most committee members assumed that most work would be conducted in the committee as a whole, but during the briefing session the need for in-depth study of special problems became evident. Consequently, PAC was divided into five standing subcommittees: housing, community planning, rehabilitation, equal opportunity and social services, and legal and bylaws. Meeting independently, each of these subcommittees carried out additional studies of their respective areas under the guidance of professional staff. Most of the detailed work of PAC was conducted through the subcommittee structure, as exemplified by the activities of the rehabilitation subcommittee.

A large amount of rehabilitation of individual dwelling units was in progress. Citizen complaints concerning this work was channeled to the rehabilitation subcommittee. These were reviewed for possible breaches of contract, poor quality of work and materials, and irresponsible acts of the contractor. Members of the subcommittee went to the construction site, inspected the property subject to the complaints, interviewed complaining parties and then made a report to the entire PAC. The report was reviewed by committee members, legal ramifications were studied by legal counsel and appropriate actions were agreed upon. Normally, administrative grievance procedures were followed first by discussing the issues with staff members of the urban renewal agency. If this did not achieve results acceptable to the committee, legal action in the courts followed. Technical advice and legal counsel were continuing needs of PAC and its various subcommittees. Indeed, PAC successes were principally dependent upon the quality and work of independent staff.

Funds to finance PAC activities were received from the urban renewal agency. These were agreed upon after consultation with local HUD officials to assure compliance with federal funding requirements as well as local guidelines. PAC controlled its own budget and the hiring of a small permanent staff. Funds were available for an executive director, a secretary, office space, publications and travel.

Technical assistance was primarily of a volunteer nature, on loan from other agencies. Legal counsel was received from the Legal Aid Society funded by the United Appeal Agency. The Neighborhood Services Organization, supported largely by contributions from the Methodist Church and from the United Appeal Agency, supplied staff assistance on relocation and social problems within the renewal area. Planning staff assistance was also voluntary, given through local university faculty and students, and from the Urban League.

The complexity of funding interrelationships is indicated by Urban League contributions. The local chapter of the Urban League received substantial support from citizen contributions to United Appeal Agency, but funding for PAC technical planning assistance was from different sources. A grant was made by HUD to the National Urban League, which, in turn, provided funds to the local affiliate of the Urban League to finance volunteer technical staff used by PAC. It is significant that PAC attained a relatively independent position since almost all funding of its activities was from federal grants or from the voluntary contributions of local citizens in their support of United Appeal programs. Local government monies that might have been subject to control by politically dominant groups with little interest in the project area were not used, thereby freeing PAC from possible influence by local groups external to the project area. The importance of this independence is illustrated by subsequent committee actions.

The first several months of PAC efforts were devoted to learning about the complexities of renewal and reviewing existing plans and renewal agency activities. As PAC members succeeded in solving some individual problems for citizens in the project area, their credibility increased throughout their constituency, and this led to an expansion of political activity. Many occupants of the project area felt that the local urban renewal agency was insensitive to the needs of project area citizens and cited what they deemed to be a long history of inequities perpetrated by a noncaring bureaucracy. Agency staff saw the increasing political muscle of PAC as a threat to plans carefully prepared in previous years and to construction in process. Communication between the groups was relatively formal, and restricted to information that was, in the words of the renewal director, "what I think the members of PAC need to know." Many questions of members remained unanswered during the first year of PAC. At the suggestion of staff, the committee took their problem directly to HUD officials in Washington. Out of this contact, a meeting among interested parties was called. Participants included PAC members and their staff representatives, local HUD representatives, and urban renewal staff. This face-to-face consultation brought into focus the common objectives of all participants and increased the respect of the renewal staff for the growing political astuteness and power of PAC.

A further demonstration of the maturity and effectiveness of PAC came in the following year, when the committee shifted from a reacting to an acting role. A planning consultant was hired by PAC to prepare a new plan for renewal of the area. The PAC plan was completed and recommended to the urban renewal agency. Subsequent reviews by affected parties led to the adoption by the city council of some of the alternatives proposed by PAC.

Several conclusions could be drawn from the work of this committee. The review and watchdog roles clearly increased the sensitivity of renewal agency staff, contractors and many others to the problems of individuals displaced or otherwise affected by renewal in the project area. The PAC provided a friendly access to a local government process that appeared to many citizens to cause precipitious action without concern for the feelings of those affected by the renewal process.

Participation in PAC provided excellent training in local government decisionmaking. It showed many who had no previous chance to be personally involved in influencing public policies affecting their lives how the system really worked. As they sat in formal sessions of PAC, members experienced the impossible task of developing programs that were equitable for all people. In the smaller, less formal meetings of subcommittees, they found out what went on behind closed doors as each vested interest group asserted the validity of its position. They learned that each member was accountable to a particular, often vocal, sometimes hostile, constituency.

Self-interest was the motivation behind most of those who initially sought membership in PAC. Composed of small businessmen and residents threatened by renewal plans, the PAC members hoped to use their position to protect personal interests in the project area, and this they did. They also discovered that knowledge and power gained in committee work could be used to help their neighbors. What frequently started as a venture in self-interest led to service for a broader constituency and a better understanding of what is meant by the public interest.

TASK FORCES

Size and Composition
The range in size of a task force is highly variable and may be as

small as fifteen or include several hundred participants. Since the principal purpose is the performance of a task, members should be selected for their interest and willingness to serve, for their special knowledge and for their capability to perform in a team effort.

Purposes and Organizational Characteristics

A task force is used to mobilize a large amount of talent for a massive effort in a major public interest area such as metropolitan planning, civil rights, open space preservation, charter revision or economic development. It may be organized to study and evaluate governmental operations, prepare and carry out action programs, or conduct a community celebration. It is an ad hoc committee that may draw membership from within and outside the community. It is frequently created to stimulate new ideas and thoughts on a subject. This may precipitate change in existing organizations and in their operational processes, but it will not usually cause basic institutional changes, since committee members tend to be leaders drawn from existing institutions. A task force usually is created by a mayor or another public official, and often will be planning, evaluation and action oriented. Some task forces may result from citizen initiatives, however, as has been the case recently in dealing with environmental issues.

Constituencies

Those who benefit from task force efforts may be a whole community or a relatively narrow segment of the population. A task force responsible for economic development may have direct and indirect impact on many different groups, while one directed toward pollution abatement on a watershed will have an entirely different type of constituency. Primary and secondary constituencies can be identified only in terms of the nature of the task that is carried out.

Resource Support Required

The type and amount of resources tends to vary widely but should be appropriate to accomplish the assigned mission. Support staff, publication expenses, travel funds and public office space may be needed for some projects, while others will be conducted almost entirely with voluntary contributions of time and other resources.

•

ILLUSTRATION

A Task Force

It was late April in a small county seat located on the eastern edge of the Great Plains. The town had a population of 4,221 persons, but the size of the business district indicated that it served a large rural trade area. Jim Goodman, sole owner and editor of the *Daily News,* which was published six evenings each week, strolled along the north side of Main Street. It was almost midmorning and he headed in the general direction of the coffee shop. A light wind stirred dust from the street. He was used to the wind, but the dust was an unconscious annoyance that pricked at the corner of his mind. Suddenly he became aware of an inconsistency. Why should there be dust on Main Street at all? The sidewalks and street surfaces were concrete. Only a longtime resident would know of the street pavement, however, since it was covered with an inch thick layer of dirt, tracked in on the wheels of countless cars and trucks that made frequent trips from surrounding farms.

As if he were seeing it for the first time, Jim looked along the four blocks lined with commercial buildings. At the west end, a wheat elevator interrupted his line of vision and formed a pleasant landmark that could be seen for miles across the plains. Near the white concrete structure of the elevator was a cluster of dilapidated frame buildings, in some of which were stored obsolete construction equipment, but most were vacant. Looking the other direction, Jim saw the large hole of an unfilled basement left two years before, the result of a fire that destroyed 200 feet of commercial frontage. The burned shell had been removed, but the buildings had not been replaced. Some store fronts were attractive; others needed remodeling and repair. The second floors of most buildings were unoccupied and some seemed strangely threatening, as if they might collapse on the occupants of the stores below. Signs and utility poles of assorted sizes, shapes and colors composed the foreground. Jim thought, "This is truly American motley. It's not a very pleasant place for people to spend their lives and something ought to be done about it."

The mayor was a hardware merchant who had grown up on a

farm, but entered business when an asthmatic condition forced his retirement from farming. Astute and well liked, he was serving an unopposed third term as mayor. He understood the needs and the slow pace of the small rural community, but his utilitarian nature made him less sensitive to community appearance.

Turning around, Jim crossed the street and entered the mayor's establishment, greeted him and gave the usual casual invitation to join in a cup of coffee. As they walked together, Jim related his thoughts of the morning and suggested that the mayor might start a clean-up campaign by having the city sanitation crew sweep Main Street. As they discussed the problem, both realized that action was long overdue, and that more than a simple cleaning task was involved.

An informal discussion with other council members resulted in a proposal that a task force be created to plan an old-fashion communitywide celebration for the Fourth of July, including a rodeo, picnics and friendly competitive sports. The celebration was to begin with a parade and end with an evening square dance on Main Street. All county citizens were to be invited. The mayor knew that it would be far more effective to have a celebration as an incentive for cleaning and refurbishing the business district than to sell the idea on its own merits. Main Street must be cleaned before it could be used for dancing.

An executive committee of the task force was appointed to plan and implement the effort. Task force participants ranged from junior high age through older adults. A massive mobilization of community resources and talent culminated in an intensive one week work effort. Over 400 tons of soil were removed from Main Street, more than enough to fill the basement hole. The burned-out area was leveled, compacted and made into a parking lot. Store fronts were painted. Eleven dilapidated buildings were removed. Seven were demolished, while four were burned under the supervision of the fire department. City equipment and staff augmented voluntary citizen labor and privately owned tractors and trucks. Twenty-eight truckloads of trash and worn out machinery were removed from the business district and nearby residential and industrial areas.

On the fifth day of July, the appearance of the community had been transformed; the day-long celebration had attracted more than 10,000 participants and left additional cleaning to be done, and perhaps most important was a strengthened community spirit that grew out of sharing hard work on a successful task. The community had the resources but needed the will to work on common tasks and the inspiration to see what those tasks should be.

Once a community spirit is generated it may prove to be a quite unpredictable and creative force. As a result of the above experience, a small group of highschool students who had participated as members of the task force noted that a large number of abandoned automobile bodies were scattered around the town. As a class project, they marked on a city map the location of each abandoned vehicle and other major accumulations of junk and trash. In the town of slightly less than two square miles, they located 164 different major deposits of trash and junk, including 337 abandoned automobile carcasses. Their findings were published in the *Daily News*, and personally reported to the city council. Although the city sanitation staff was small, through a concerted effort all of the mapped sites of junk were cleared in less than a year, and an effective countywide solid waste disposal system was started.

Each community will have to decide for itself what kinds of jobs are appropriate for task forces and work groups, and what strategies will be most effective in carrying out such tasks. The opportunities for generating community service through use of volunteer citizen efforts are almost limitless, restricted only by the initiative and vision of community leaders.

WORK GROUPS

Size and Composition

Highly variable in size, a work group may range from five to 300 or more citizens. The principle requirement for membership is to be willing and capable of carrying out the assigned task.

Purpose and Organization

The work group, like the task force, is normally organized to voluntarily perform a specific job or carry out a project. The difference between the two types tends to be one of degree. Both are ad hoc organizations, but a task force normally performs more complex assignments requiring greater time and talent. A work group is a contemporary counterpart of the banding together of neighbors of an earlier era for barn raising, church construction, or other community or personal service projects using voluntary shared labor. Work groups form a convenient arrangement for enlisting short-term labor from many sources. Youth organizations such as Scouts and Camp-fire Girls are frequently recruited as work groups for community clean-up, pollution abatement, tree planting and other public interest projects. The roles performed by members of both task forces and work groups are counter to the general rule that committee assignments should not be substituted for paid staff. Work groups often perform services that would be quite costly if staff were hired; thus, a substantial savings in public funds may be realized. The cleaning of debris from a polluted stream may generate unacceptably high costs if city staff performs the services. As an alternative, the job may be effectively and enthusiastically accomplished by organizing a large work group of citizens committed to cleaning up the environment. Public recognition of committee efforts is especially important, particularly where young members are involved. Satisfaction gained in performing public tasks may be the stimulus for increased public service in later years.

Constituencies

The discussions of task force constituencies apply equally to work groups. The community frequently is the primary constituency, but the nature of each task that is performed will dictate the principal recipients of committee efforts.

Resource Support Required

The types of resources required will depend upon the type of project. Tasks requiring large amounts of manual labor may require transportation to the site of the project and funds for food or refreshments. Other assignments may require special equipment, office space and support staff. Those initiating the committee effort should identify the types of resources needed and their availability in advance planning stages of the project. Work groups and task forces have been particularly active in recent years cleaning up the natural environment. A number of case studies of citizen organization efforts have been published and are available from the Environmental Protection Agency.[9]

Chapter 6

Future Prospects for
Citizen Committees

As a guide for persons who serve as members or are responsible for creating them, citizen committees have been
grouped under seven major headings. Within this typology,
thirteen different types of committees have been described in some
detail according to origin, purpose and organizational structure. For
ease of reference, a summary of committee characteristics is given in
Appendix A. While there is no survey of the number and variety of
citizen committees that exist within the United States today, it
seems safe to assume that, so long as democracy thrives, committee
usage will continue to expand in direct proportion to the increase in
population and urbanization. Several factors appear to support this
assumption.

Clearly, citizen committees have proved to be highly beneficial
units of organization for accomplishing many purposes. Of singular
importance has been the educational impact of participation on a
committee. Each individual member, in working cooperatively on a
task with other citizens, tends to gain new knowledge of the community and of its people. Committees have provided excellent training
for those who desire to move on to more advanced levels of public
responsibility in elective or appointive public offices. And, for those
participants who go no farther than volunteer service on a committee, there is both the renewal of awareness of the complexities of the
community in which they live and an increased sensitivity for the
different, often competing, interest groups that compose even a relatively small human settlement.

A summary of other benefits, previously identified, which are derived from citizen committees, includes the fact that committees tend to increase public access to the decisionmaking process and provide mechanisms for cooperation and communication among people of different backgrounds who have common interests. They offer avenues for minority involvement and leadership training. Committees also may serve as conduits to channel the special talents and training of individuals to benefit public programs. They provide a forum where ideas and concepts can be tested, where political power is made more visible, and where issues are brought into sharper focus. Finally, the use of citizen committees tends to "open up" the process of public decisionmaking by reducing partisanship and fixing accountability for official actions. As committee participation expands the opportunity for the governed to participate meaningfully in the government, the greater will be the tendency toward a government that is responsive to each citizen.

Citizen committees seem to be especially adaptable to the institution of American local government. Often, they form the link that ties together and gives unity to private and public efforts. The proposal to locate a new civic center involves a variety of public considerations and may generate intense competition among different private economic interests. A citizens planning or advisory committee may offer an effective mechanism for resolving differences among these varying interest groups. Moreover, the widespread use of the ad hoc citizen committee may be a most effective instrument in preventing local governments from becoming top heavy bureaucracies. Alvin Toffler has identified the increasing use of ad hoc organizations as a new approach to problem solving.[1] In local governments the ad hoc committee is being employed increasingly to deal with a specific problem; when solved, the committee goes out of existence. In contrast, the creation of a massive civil service, as an alternative, would force the expansion of permanent staff and add to the cost of government.

As numerical increases in population occur, and social and economic problems become more complex, there seems to be an inherent tendency toward the centralization of power at the national level, with a consequent diminution of the ability of government to respond to the daily needs of people. Indeed, if democracy as we have known it in America is to survive in a healthy state, power must be continuously channeled downward and diffused among its citizenry. Citizen participation, which has been deemed inherently desirable in the past, may be an imperative for the future.

Citizens may be expected to continue their involvement as long as democracy really works, and they may frequently act both to retard and to contribute to the processes of growth and of change that are a constant mark of human communities. Citizen committees, carefully organized and supplied with sufficient resources, can be highly creative forces in the difficult task of community building. The opportunities for generating local initiative and accomplishing public work through volunteer citizen efforts are almost limitless, restricted only by the ingenuity and vision of community leaders.

✳

Postscript

As government structures evolve to meet the new social and technological demands of the decade of the 1980s which is almost upon us, citizen committees may take a variety of new forms, and old forms may be used in new ways. The typology and illustrations recounted here may be useful models for a long time to come, but you, the reader, will undoubtedly become involved in many experiences with committees. If you discover a new or innovative approach taken by a citizen committee, or any form of citizen participation, I would appreciate having a written account so that it can be considered for inclusion in a revised edition when warranted by new information. Please mail accounts to the author at 650 Parrington Oval, University of Oklahoma, Norman, Oklahoma 73019.

J.L.R.

✳

Appendix A

**Summary of Citizen Committee
Characteristics by Type, Purpose
and Organizational Structure**

✳

Appendix B

(These are the Bylaws of a highly successful community council that has been in continuous operation in Norman, Oklahoma, since September 1959)

ARTICLE I—NAME
Section 1—The name of this organization shall be the CIVIC IMPROVEMENT COUNCIL OF NORMAN.
Section 2—This organization shall be an unincorporated association, conducting its principal activities within the city of Norman, Oklahoma.

ARTICLE II—OBJECTIVE
Section 1—The fundamental purpose of this organization shall be to work for the continued improvement of all aspects of the community of Norman, Oklahoma.
Section 2—It shall be the responsibility of this organization to receive factual information pertaining to various problems, to make recommendations, and to assist in the presentation and communication of these facts and recommendations to all citizens of the community.

ARTICLE III—LIMITATION OF METHODS
Section 1—The Council shall be nonpartisan and nonsectarian and shall take no part in or lend its influence or facilities, either directly or indirectly, to the nomination, election or appointment of any candidate for office in city, county, state or nation.

ARTICLE IV—MEMBERSHIP

Section 1—Membership in the organization is open to all functioning civic, service and community groups who desire to work for betterment of the Norman community. Each participating group shall select three members (one of whom must be the president or his designated representative) to serve as members of the organization.

Section 2—The membership committee shall make recommendations to the board of directors as to additional citizens whom it regards as worthy of membership at large. The board of directors may extend invitations to such recommended citizens to become members at large of the council. The term of membership of a member at large shall be for one year unless such membership be renewed by invitation of the board of directors, and such renewal shall only be authorized by the board of directors after recommendation by the membership committee.

Section 3—Each member at large in good standing, and each representative of a participating civic club or organization, shall be entitled to one vote as an individual on any matter to be determined by vote of the membership of the council.

Section 4—There shall be no dues for membership in the council, but the council shall accept contributions from the various organizations represented. The representatives of each participating organization shall encourage financial support toward the work of the council from their organization which they represent. Contributions from members at large may be accepted in such amounts as the board of directors may determine from time to time.

Section 5—No more than one-third (1/3) of the entire number of individuals constituting the membership of the council shall be members at large at any time. Members at large shall be eligible to hold office in the council.

ARTICLE V—MEETINGS

Section 1—This organization shall hold a regular meeting at 7:30 P.M. on the fourth Monday of each month. Special meetings may be held upon call of the president, or upon written request of any five (5) members of the council. Special meetings shall be called a sufficient time in advance of the meeting that due notice thereof may be given by publication in the newspaper and by radio.

Section 2—A quorum at any meeting of the membership of the council shall be a majority of the members of the council. when a quorum is present, a majority vote of those present shall be sufficient to adopt any motion or transact any other business for the council.

ARTICLE VI—BOARD OF DIRECTORS

Section 1—The board of directors shall meet in regular session in advance of each monthly meeting of the organization and shall be responsible for the preparation of the agenda.

Section 2—Decisions as to the order of importance of projects to be undertaken by this organization shall be made by the members of the council.

Section 3—The board of directors shall be composed of one representative from each participating organization, together with the executive committee of the council. The president of the council shall preside at meetings of the board of directors.

Section 4—A majority of the membership of the board of directors shall constitute a quorum at any meeting of the board. A majority vote of those present at a meeting of the board of directors at which meeting a quorum is present shall be sufficient to transact business.

Section 5—The board of directors shall function as the planning body for the organization.

ARTICLE VII—OFFICERS

Section 1—This organization shall have elected officers as follows: president, first vice-president, second vice-president, secretary and treasurer.

Section 2—The elected officers shall comprise the executive committee of the council.

Section 3—*ELECTION OF OFFICERS:* At the monthly meeting

in September of each year, the above officers shall be elected to serve for one year and until their successors are elected and qualified. At the meeting preceding such September meeting, the president shall appoint a nominating committee from names of members submitted to him by the board of directors, and such nominating committee shall, at the September meeting, present to the membership its nominations for the respective offices above mentioned, to be filled by the election at the September meeting. The nominating committee shall consist of three members of the council.

Nominations from the floor for each office may be made at the September meeting, prior to the election.

Section 4—The president shall preside at all meetings of the membership and of the board of directors and shall perform all duties incident to the office. He shall appoint all committees subject to the approval of the board of directors. He shall be the ex officio member of all committees. He shall at such times as he may deem proper commend to the membership and/or the board of director such matters and make such suggestions as may tend to promote the purposes of the council.

Section 5—The first vice-president shall act in the absence of the president.

Section 6—The second vice-president shall act in the absence of the president and the first vice-president.

Section 7—The secretary shall conduct the official correspondence; preserve all books, documents and communications; and maintain or cause to be maintained an accurate record of the proceedings of the council, the board of directors and the executive committee. He shall keep or cause to be kept such other necessary records as the board of directors may determine.

Section 8—The treasurer shall receive and disburse the funds of the council. He shall make reports to the board of directors at least annually, and more often if the board shall require.

Section 9—In the interim between meetings of the board of directors, the executive committee shall have charge of the routine business of the council. It shall have general charge of the finances and the property of the council and shall have authority to order disbursements for necessary expenses. All action taken by the executive committee shall be reported to the board of directors. The executive committee shall have such other responsibilities and be vested with such other powers as the board of directors may determine.

ARTICLE VIII—COMMITTEES

Section 1—The board of directors shall authorize and define the powers and duties of all committees.

Section 2—The president shall appoint all committees subject to confirmation by the board of directors. Each committee member shall serve during the pleasure of the president.

Section 3—No committee, standing or special, shall have the power to commit the council on any matter of general policy. No committee shall spend or obligate funds in excess of the amount allocated to it by the board of directors or the executive committee.

Section 4—Committee meetings may be called at any time by the chairman of the committee, or by the president.

Section 5—In the event any committee fails to discharge the duties assigned to it with reasonable promptness, such committee may be discharged by the president, who shall report his action to the board of directors and thereupon appoint a new committee.

Section 6—The committees of the council shall consist of the following: streets and storm sewers; safety; city beautification; library facilities; parks and playgrounds; youth; sanitation; annexation; governmental relations; membership; and such other committees as the board of directors may determine to be necessary.

ARTICLE IX—DISBURSEMENTS

Section 1—No disbursement of the funds of the council shall be made unless the same shall have been approved, authorized and ordered by the board of directors or the executive committee.

Section 2—All disbursements shall be made by check. Checks shall be signed by the treasurer and countersigned by the president.

ARTICLE X—BUDGET

Section 1—The annual budget of the council shall be prepared by the board of directors, or by a committee appointed by the board of directors for that purpose, and shall be subject to approval by the membership of the council.

ARTICLE XI—FISCAL YEARS

Section 1—The fiscal year shall begin on the first day of October in each year and end on the 30th day of September of the following year.

ARTICLE XII—PARLIAMENTARY PROCEDURE

Section 1—The proceedings of meetings of the council shall be governed by and conducted according to the latest edition of Roberts Manual of Parliamentary Rules.

ARTICLE XIII—AMENDMENTS

Section 1—These bylaws may be amended or altered by two-thirds (2/3) vote of a quorum present at any regular or special meeting of the membership of the council, provided that notice of the proposed change shall have been given either by mail to each member of the council at least thirty days prior to the date of such meeting, or by verbal announcement at the preceding regular monthly meeting of the council.

Notes

CHAPTER I

1. Alexis de Tocqueville, *Democracy in America*, translated by Phillip Bradley (New York: Alfred A. Knopf, Inc., 1945).

2. A. Hale Vandermer, "The Development of a Methodology to Evaluate the Availability and Utilization of Health Care Resources" Ph.D. dissertation, University of Oklahoma, Norman, 1975), pp. 82, 83.

3. Department of Housing and Urban Development, Rules and Regulations, "Community Development Block Grants," *Federal Register*, vol. 39, no. 220, pt. III, November 13, 1974, p. 40150, sec. 570.907(b).

4. National Model Cities Community Development Directors Association, *A Guide to Meeting Citizen Participation Requirements for Community Development* Washington, D.C., February 1975), p. 6.

5. Arthur J. Vidich and Joseph Bensman, *Small Towns in Mass Society*, (Princeton: Princeton University Press, 1968), p. 23.

6. M. L. Wilson, "A Theory of Agricultural Democracy" (Address before the American Political Science Association, Chicago December 28, 1940). Published as an Extension Service Circular 355, March 1941 (Mimeo.), and in Philip Selznick, *TVA and the Grass Roots* (New York: Harper & Row, 1966), p. 222.

7. Ibid.

8. Gordon R. Clapp served as the second director of TVA, following David E. Lillienthol.

9. James Dahir, *Region Building* (New York: Harper and Brothers, 1955), p. 17.

10. "The Annual Report of the Council of Economic Advisors," Economic Report to the President, January 1969, p. 153.

11. For a comprehensive discussion of federal programs for rural America, see James L. Sundquist and David W. Davis, *Making Federalism Work*, (Washington, D.C.: The Brookings Institute, 1969), pp. 130–66.

12. Ibid., p. 133.

13. Ibid., pp. 144–45.

14. For information on citizen participation see William C. Loring, Jr., Frank L. Sweetser, and Charles F. Ernst, *Community Organization for Citizen Participation in Urban Renewal*, prepared by Housing Association of Metropolitan Boston, Inc. (Cambridge, Massachusetts: The Cambridge Press, Inc., 1957); Planning and Citizen Participation, *The Journal of the American Institute of Planners* XXXXV, no. 4, (July, 1969); International City Managers Association, "Public Involvement in Local Government in the 1970's," *Management Information Service Report*, 6, no. 1 (January 1974).

CHAPTER TWO

1. For a case study and analysis of citizen committees required under federal programs, see Melvin B. Mogulof, *Citizen Participation: The Local Perspective* (Washington, D.C.: The Urban Institute, 1973).

2. Ibid., p. 68. For a recent account of minority participation see National Urban League, *Toward Effective Citizen Participation in Urban Renewal* (New York, 1973).

3. Mogulof, pp. 19–20.

4. Ibid.

5. Sherry R. Arnstein, "A Ladder of Citizen Participation," *Journal of The American Institute of Planners* XXXV, no. 4 (July 1969): 216–24.

CHAPTER FIVE

1. Melvin B. Mogulof, *Citizen Participation: The Local Perspective*, (Washington, D.C.: The Urban Institute, 1973), pp. 12–18.

2. Ibid., p. 96.

3. Goals Committee Report *Goals of Cupertino* (Cupertino, California: Office of the Mayor, 1973), pp. i–ii.

4. See Los Angeles Goals Council Report, *Summary Report of the Los Angeles Goal Council* (Los Angeles, November 1969). For information on Corups, Christi, Texas, program, contact the Department of City Planning, Municipal Building.

5. For an illustration of a sample survey used in a goals formulation program see *Summary Report of the Los Angeles Goals Council*, Appendix 1.

6. Although twenty-eight months may seem to be a fairly long time period for goals study, both the subject and the process are complex and time-consuming, even for a small community. Larger cities may require several years to develop the first phase of a comprehensive goals program, which then may involve almost continuous review and updating. The Los Angeles Goals Council required more than five years to prepare its 1969 goals report.

8. Facts supplied by Jess Abrams.

9. See *A Citizens Solid Waste Management Project: Mission 5000* (1972), *Don't Leave it all to the Experts* (1972), and *Citizen Action Can Get Results*

(1972), Environmental Protection Agency, Published by the Office of Public Affairs, Washington, D.C. Also see Citizens Advisory Committee on Environmental Quality, *Citizens Make the Difference, Case Studies of Environmental Action* (Washington, DC.: U.S. Government Printing Office, 1973).

CHAPTER SIX

1. Alvin Toffler, *Future Shock* (New York: Random House, Bantam Edition, 1971), pp. 134–35.

※

Bibliography

Books

American Society of Planning Officials. *Planning 1958*. Chicago, 1958.

Biddle, William W. *The Cultivation of Community Leaders: Up From the Grass Roots*. New York: Harper and Brothers, 1959.

Cole, Richard L. *Citizen Participation and the Urban Policy Process*. Lexington, Mass.: Lexington Books, 1973.

Dahir, James. *Region Building*. New York: Harper and Brothers, 1955.

Goodman, William I., ed. *Principles and Practice of Urban Planning*. 4th ed. Washington, D.C.: International City Managers' Association, 1968.

Harper, Ernest B., and Dunham, Arthur. *Community Organization in Action*. New York: Association Press, 1959.

Hillman, Arthur. *Community Organization and Planning*. New York: Macmillan Publisher, 1950.

Loring, William C., Jr.; Sweetser, Frank L.; and Ernst, Charles F. *Community Organization for Citizen Participation in Urban Renewal*. Prepared by Housing Association of Metropolitan Boston, Inc., for the Massachusetts Department of Commerce. Cambridge, Massachusetts: The Cambridge Press, Inc., 1957.

Mogulof, Melvin B. *Citizen Participation: The Local Perspective*. Washington, D.C.: The Urban Institute, 1973.

Selznick, Philip. *TVA and the Grass Roots*. New York: Harper and Row, 1966.

Sundquist, James L., and Davis, David W. *Making Federalism Work*. Washington, D.C.: The Brookings Institution, 1969.

Webb, Kenneth, and Hatry, Harry P. *Obtaining Citizen Feedback: The Application of Citizen Surveys to Local Governments*. Washington, D.C.: The Urban Institute, 1973.

99

Periodicals and Journals

Arnstein, Sherry. "A Ladder of Citizen Participation." *Journal of the American Institute of Planners* XXXV, no. 4 (July 1969): 216–24.

Bourgeois, A. Donald. "Citizen's Role in St. Louis Model Cities Program Described." *Journal of Housing* 11 (December 1967): 613–14.

Burke, Edmund M. "Citizen Participation Strategies." *Journal of the American Institute of Planners* XXXIV, no. 5 (September 1968): 287–94.

English, G. "The Trouble with Community Action." *Public Administration Review* XXXII (May 1972): 224–31.

Esser, George H., Jr. "Involving the Citizen in Decision-Making." *Nation's Cities* VI, no. 5 (May 1968):11–14.

Goltschaik, Shimon. "Citizen Participation in the Development of New Towns: A Cross-National View." *Social Service Review* XXXXV, no. 2 (June 1971): 194–204.

Hyman, Herbert. "Planning with Citizens: Two Styles." *Journal of the American Institute of Planners* XXXV, no. 2 (March 1969): pp. 105–12.

International City Management Association. "Public Involvement in Local Government in the 1970's," *Management Information Service Report* 6, no. 1 (January 1974).

Mogulof, Melvin B. "Coalition to Adversary: Citizen Participation in Three Federal Programs." *Journal of the American Institute of Planners* XXXV (1969): 225–32.

Neighborhood Decentralization. Washington, D.C.: Center for Governmental Studies, March-April 1975.

"Planning and Citizen Participation: Costs, Benefits, and Approaches." *The Urban Affairs Quarterly*, June 1970, p. 369.

Siegel, Roberta. "Citizen Advisory Groups." *Nation's Cities* VI, no. 5 (May 1968): 15–21.

Strange, J. H. "Citizen Participation in Community Action and Model Cities Programs." *Public Administration Review* XXXII (October 1972): pp. 655–69.

Theodore, E. D., et al. "Citizen Awareness and Involvement in Poverty Action." *Social Problems* IXX (Spring 1972): 484–89.

Published Materials

Citizens' Advisory Committee on Environmental Quality. *Citizens Make the Difference, Case Studies of Environmental Action.* Washington, D.C.: U.S. Government Printing Office, January 1973.

Environmental Protection Agency. *Citizen Action Can Get Results.* Washington, D.C., August 1972.

——. *A Citizens' Solid Waste Management Project: Mission 5000.* Washington, D.C., 1972.

——. *Citizen Suits Under the Clean Air Act.* Washington, D.C., 1972.

——. Office of Public Affairs. *Don't Leave It All to the Experts.* Washington, D.C., November 1972.

Goals Committee Report. *Goals of Cupertino.* Cupertino, California: Office of the Mayor, April 1973.

Los Angeles Goals Council. *Summary Report of the Los Angeles Goals Council.* Los Angeles, November 1969.

Maffin, Robert W.; Silverman, Edward; Sosson, Deena. *For Plotting a Local Community Development Course* (Chart Book). Washington, D.C.: National Association of Housing and Redevelopment Officials, January 1975.

National Urban League, Urban Renewal Demonstration Project. *Toward Effective Citizen Participation in Urban Renewal.* New York, 1973.

✳

About the Author

Joseph Lee Rodgers, Jr. is Professor of Regional and City Planning at the University of Oklahoma, Norman, where for the past fifteen years he has served as Chairman of the graduate professional program of planning and as Director of the Oklahoma Center of Urban and Regional Studies. He received professional degrees in Civil Engineering in 1946, and in Planning in 1953, from the University of Oklahoma, and has been an active planning practitioner for more than thirty years. He has directed and authored numerous comprehensive planning studies for city, metropolitan, state and regional agencies throughout the Southwest. He has written several widely used model planning acts, housing codes, zoning ordinances, and subdivision regulations. His most recent work is another book published by Ballinger Publishing Company entitled *Environmental Impact Assessment, Growth Management and the Comprehensive Plan*, 1976. A native Oklahoman who resides with his wife and four children in Norman, he also has traveled widely throughout the United States to lecture and conduct research on a broad range of urban issues.